Mysteries of the Light Revealed

Mysteries of the Light Revealed

ALL YOU WANT TO KNOW ABOUT LIFE ON THE OTHER SIDE

CHANNELED INSIGHTS SERIES
BOOK ONE

JULIE BAWDEN-DAVIS

BHAGWAN SHREE RAJNEESH

Roses
ARE
RED
PUBLISHING

Cover by Judy Bullard (customebookcovers.com)

Gemstone logo by Jeremy Davis

Book design by Julie Bawden-Davis

Roses are Red logo design by Kyle Kane

ISBN 13: 978-1-955265-47-8

ISBN 10: 1-955265-47-X

Distributed by Roses Are Red Publishing

rosesareredpublishing.com

Dedication

For all those who live in the Light, long for the Light and will enter the Light when they leave planet Earth. This is for you, with our love from the Light.

Preface

There are times in our lives when an individual or circumstance presents and pieces of the puzzle of our life slide into place. Prior to Shobha Cameron finding me, Julie Bawden-Davis, on the Web in 2021, I had received intimations from Spirit that an important spiritual project was on its way, and it was intricately tied to my life purpose. At the time, I had no idea in what form this significant experience would come about. I just knew that I would know when the situation or person appeared.

When Shobha contacted me, I had recently published the first four books in my Channeled Masters Series, which features channeled messages from well-known people who have passed into the Light. Although I have channeled (translated messages from the Light/Multiverse into written and spoken form) since I started writing at the age of 5, it was not until I penned the Channeled Masters Series that I discovered I am a Master Channeler.

This information came from Spirit, as well as through some highly gifted psychics and mediums. It was explained to me that after channeling over many lifetimes, I had achieved the ability to tap into just about any frequency or entity and hear, comprehend, translate, and record what is being communicated. To be a Master

Channeler, a person must also be trusted by the Light to accurately relay the information received and protect its integrity.

When I received the message about being a Master Channeler, everything suddenly fell perfectly into place for me. I realized that one of my soul missions is to channel inspiring, informative, and healing messages from the Light so that people can understand what occurs in the "Great Beyond," also known as "Beyond the Veil" and "The Other Side." One of the most important messages that comes forth through this channeling is that there truly is no death.

It was on January 27, 2021, that Shobha first contacted me via email. She had found my website and felt an immediate connection when she saw my photo and read about my experiences since childhood with the spiritual world.

As an anthropologist and writer, Shobha's spiritual quest began when she was eleven years old. In 1973, she began to seek a living enlightened master on Earth to guide her—having already explored many spiritual paths up until that time. Three years later, she happened to pick up the book, *The Way of the White Clouds*, based on the talks of Bhagwan Shree Rajneesh (also known as Osho). She immediately knew that "this was it." Within a few days, she had sold her possessions (including her beloved piano) and left for India—where she was initiated by Bhagwan as his sannyasin.

In the late 1970s, Bhagwan's ashram in Pune, India was attracting many seekers from western countries who were searching for spiritual understanding. Fifty years later in 2024, his books, tapes and videos are now read, heard and watched by millions in India and around the globe.

When Shobha and I met, she had already published *Kissing the Joy as it Flies – Letters to the Beloved* in 2017, based on 3,500 love letters with her soulmate, Douglas Payne, over thirty years on Earth. When Douglas slipped sideways in 2016 at the age of 94, Shobha was also inspired to publish *You Belong to the Stars* in 2021. The book is based on monthly sessions over five years involving messages channeled from the Light from Bhagwan and Douglas to Shobha—by medium Peta Anderson. (Bhagwan had himself passed into the Light in 1990). *You Belong to the Stars* was a novice attempt by Shobha to pass on her perception of the Light as given by Bhagwan and Douglas.

Bhagwan and Shobha had discussed the possibility of channeling a book based upon what it is like—on the Other Side— from the Other Side. They conferred together and subsequently with me to see if we could bring the project to fruition. It was then I realized that this was the spiritual project I had been informed by Spirit to anticipate.

So, in August 2022, I began channeling this book from Bhagwan and his "team" in the Light with continual cross-referencing between the parties involved. The project took a little more than two years, as it was channeled slowly over time. This occurred because the vibrational energy I received during channeling from the Ascended Masters in the Light was at a very high frequency level of spiritual understanding.

In addition to hearing from Bhagwan—who is the primary contributor to this work—within these pages you will read channeled messages from other Ascended Masters in the Light.

And so, the link between Earth and the Light has been forged in print once again—and continues—with the publication of *Mysteries of the Light Revealed*.

My hope is that you gain inspiration and encouragement from the words you find here, as well as an enduring understanding that we are never truly alone. A vast network of souls in the Light is always there to provide guidance for us. We need only ask.

Julie Bawden-Davis
Orange, California
November 2024

I am Bhagwan. You may also know me as Osho, because since my departure from earth in 1990, my words—spoken and recorded over a period of more than fifteen years—have been disseminated throughout the globe in hundreds of books, videos, and CDs to those interested in exploring their inner light and understanding the wider purpose of the Cosmos and their place within it.

Some grand concepts will be discussed within these pages that will be unfamiliar to you, but you may nevertheless find many of your questions answered about why we are here at all.

This book was completed through a Master Channeler by a group of four of us who are—for want of a better description— on the Other Side, Beyond the Veil, in the Great Beyond, in the Light. We have left our human mortal bodies and wish to share with you some of the wisdom and glory of what life is like once you exit planet Earth.

You may ask why we have come to Earth at this time to speak to you through a Master Channeler, who has a lifetime of experience.

Firstly, because it is time. Secondly, this is the first time a channeler with such extensive ability and experience has been available.

We are truly blessed, but it is also true that it has been divinely orchestrated that Julie is able to be with us for this purpose.

We will together offer you a glimpse—a bird's eye view—of the Other Side located beside you in the "sideways" dimension. It is not far away. Nevertheless, despite its proximity, we will also give you an overall sense of how the Universe operates.

We also wish to let you know a few home truths. First, and perhaps most importantly, you cannot die. You will never die and will live forever—albeit, not necessarily in human form. This may be a formidable prospect for some of you who hope to cease upon the midnight, as the English poet John Keats so aptly puts it. For others, it may be a delight and confirmation of your greatest wishes.

We have four voices in our team, but as we have progressed with each chapter, we have found a gentle way into your minds and hearts that will resonate closely with you and your life in the twenty-first century, now at the mercy of artificial intelligence.

We will explain why you are here; what you are potentially able to experience while you are here, and what will happen when you eventually leave your body and slip sideways. For those of you who have had any acquaintance with mediums or psychics on Earth, this will not come as a surprise. For those who adhere to a particular religion that accepts continuity of the spirit, this is also not a revelation. Such adherents have always hoped for such an outcome, even if they have no direct experience of the beyond that they can recall.

For those on Earth who wish to understand what happens when you slip sideways or shuffle off your mortal coil, as Shakespeare has expressed this phenomenon, there are many such references to surrendering the body to a fate unknown—but little description of what happens next. So, you continue to live in a kind of void until you too experience illness or old age and make the ultimate journey. Some of you are literally hanging on for dear life, and others wish with all their hearts to end it all.

But the Cosmos has a life of its own and has no limits—think infinity. You will always be here in one form or another. In fact, the Cosmos is so vast, it is almost not worth mentioning—as it is beyond your comprehension at present.

So, we have "watered down" some of our original thoughts about transmitting to you details of how we operate in the Light —as we call it. That is, the realm which all those currently not in human form inhabit. Some of you may decide to return to Earth at a later date after you slip sideways. Some of you have ties with humans on Earth and may wish to see them again. But if you wait a little, you will probably meet them again when they come over to the Other Side—which could be a preferable option. If you do decide to make the reverse trip back to earth at some stage, you may be able to pass on to others your understanding of the Great Beyond and its purpose.

So, upon reflection, our first grandiose words have been adapted for those of you who were reborn on Earth in time for the revolution in social consciousness of the sixties and seventies —when anything seemed possible. Your values were reassessed and many new ideas emerged that advocated freedom of thought and action and being—contrary to the rigid expectations of the past.

In many countries, those on Earth are now able to follow their own inclinations, but there are still those enslaved by their inherited beliefs and are not yet free.

We are here to reveal to you a Universe that espouses free will and loving kindness towards others—above all else. When you enter the Light at the end of your human life, your purpose for being here on Earth at this time will become more apparent to you, and you will be enveloped in the love of those who have been on the same journey and found understanding.

We encourage you to keep reading until you can no longer absorb any more—for now at least. I hope you can come with us, so the veil that may be obscuring your vision will fall away.

We have endeavored to express ourselves in a language that is easily understood by the present generations on Earth able to take the plunge, as it were, and enter the domain of the mystics—who have always said there was something out there, but which we say is not only out there, but in here—in your own being—if you care to open your heart.

Know that you will be fuller in your knowing by reading this. Truly, you will be guided home to you along your soul journey.

We in the Light are blessed that our writings have found their way into your hearts, so we can share our vision of the Universe with you and all who wish to live in the world of the Divine.

Our love is with you—until we meet again.

Bhagwan

P.S.

This tome of wisdom is rather heady and can be a bit overwhelming at times as the human mind strives to understand and even adapt to the contents within. You will likely have a more satisfying and enlightening experience if you heed your inner compass when your inner compass says it is time to stop reading for a while. We suggest you consider reading this in bite-size pieces if you find you are becoming overwhelmed or even confused. When you return, things will likely fall into place for you.

P.P.S.

When I was on Earth, I did not speak of the "Other Side." At that time, it seemed more important to bring your focus back to the present, not wonder about what would happen when you leave your bodies. But now the time is ripe to let you into the mysteries of the other side; to inform you that you can never die. You will live forever. In our book, *You belong to the Stars,* we began a conversation with you about what the Other Side is "like," so that you can prepare a little, and not be so overwhelmed by the beauty of it all. It will be very different from the life you are living now on Earth, but there will be many similarities.

This book is a beginning—an introduction if you will—and there is much to learn. If I was on Earth now, I would have revealed some of the mysteries of the life to come when you leave your bodies, but that opportunity is no longer available, so in this book, we will together enter into what is at present unknown territory for you unless you are one of the blessed few who interact on a daily or occasional basis with those on the Other Side. But this is rare, and there are few indeed who have been blessed to have been given such insights.

Here we offer you the insight, with the assurance that the world of Spirit/The Light offers pure bliss and contentment. There is no sadness in The Light. Only the chance to at last find meaning that is eternal.

—Bhagwan Shree Rajneesh (aka Osho)

Disclaimer. This is a channeled work that has been delivered from the Light to the EarthPlane via a Master Channeler. While this work is quite extensive and inclusive of what occurs here in the Light, it is not a complete account. For, just as things are constantly changing on the EarthPlane, so are things changing in the Light. However, what is explained and expounded upon here still holds true.

The Path of the Soul and The Stages of Ascension

PART ONE

To begin our overview of the journey of the Soul, we will attempt to give you a picture of the world of Light in all its glory. That way you can begin to understand (and perhaps remember) how life is lived on the Other Side. You will be experiencing this again when you "slip sideways," as we call it, as you left the Light behind when you chose to come to Earth and those memories were temporarily erased.

There are also others here chiming in from time to time and adding their contributions. Each member of our team speaking to you now, including myself (Bhagwan), is a being or Soul in the Light. The time has come to transmit our understanding to you, so that you may be able to interact with us while you are on Earth, and to prepare you for when you again cross to the Other Side.

By having this understanding now, you will be able to live in and foster in others, harmony with the aspirations of the Light, while you are still living your Earthly existence. You will also be enabled to more easily make the transition from your Earthly reality to the world of Light when the time is right for each one of you to come "home" to the Light.

In view of my recent lifetime on Earth, and as an Ascended Master, I am helping those on Earth reading this book understand the relationship between Earth and the Light at this critical juncture in Earth's evolution.

THE EARTH BODY

The EarthPlane, as you know, is the plane on which the physical body exists and resides. The LightPlane is the plane where the soul resides and there is no physical body.

The Earth body you currently inhabit is a carbon-based vehicle used by humans to house their souls so they may function on the EarthPlane. When a soul becomes one with an Earth body, it identifies with that body.

However, the Soul is NOT OF THE EARTH, and this bears repeating. The Earth body is nothing more than a vessel, but it is a useful vehicle to get you from point A to point B. You maintain the vehicle so it does not break down. Similarly, it is necessary to have an Earth body in good functioning order.

It is critical to treat the Earth body well so it can work at its utmost. However, it is not necessary or possible to BECOME the body, yet many find they confuse their identity with the physical body. Those living the EarthPlane existence may be driven, for example, to ensure the physical body is what they consider ideal through practices such as plastic surgery. There is nothing "wrong" with a soul wishing to look his or her best while on the EarthPlane, but there is an important distinction here—the physical body is not the soul. It is merely a vessel that transports one through the human existence.

Whereas the EarthPlane body is carbon-based, the soul is made of millions of electrical currents. When in the Light, those currents create lightning bolts or surges of light you can equate with a thought—each thought enabling souls to telepathically communicate with one another. When two souls in the Light know each other well, they telepathically communicate with one another without the need for lightning bolts, but energy still passes between them.

At this juncture, we suggest you make a strong cup of coffee or take a nap to fortify you for what is to come, as there is much to digest that may be unfamiliar.

HIERARCHY IN THE LIGHT

There is a definite hierarchy in the Light. You may wish to think that no one is above anyone else and we are all "equal" when on the Other Side. While it is true that no one is "better" than anyone else, there are differences in how far souls have come in their understanding and assimilation of the infinite possibilities in the Light. This level of understanding and assimilation affects the roles for which they are best suited.

You may be asking why hierarchy is necessary in the Light of all places? It is a notion that would seem to suit those on Earth rather than those in the Light. The simple principle of attraction or "like attracts like" is a partial explanation. Those who work with the same or a similar level of understanding are those that a soul is best suited to be with.

It is not a question of some being "better than others." It is a matter of difference in the ways we ascend in understanding. We cannot all be mathematicians or scientists. We cannot all be poets or musicians—even on Earth.

You may not be able to identify yourself as yet within the LightPlane hierarchical scheme. If you are able, that is wonderful, but it is not necessary at this time. It will become apparent in due course. Even if you think you know where you fit, you may not be correct.

The Soul Ascension Path is not a straight line. Rather, it can take many zigs and zags along the way. That being said, it isn't something you have to worry yourself about—for all the zigs and the zags go exactly where they are meant to go. Does this mean the process is not well designed? On the contrary, the process is what you would call a planned, methodical one. The zigs and zags allow for the "unexpected" and changes in plans. So, everything is planned but may not appear to be so.

Let us give you an example. Your soul wishes to learn the lesson of faith and trust in all that has been planned and preordained. While this may seem like a straightforward process, it is not the case, because the "greater" the lesson, the more challenges there will be on the journey.

There are also many stops and starts along your soul path. At times you may feel a "stall" and wonder what is happening, or perhaps even more so, what is not happening and why? To explain such pauses, we must first look at the body in its human form. Sometimes the body "wears out" and requires rest and maintenance. So, this can be a reason for a slowdown. The body needs to rest and catch up. At other times, the human mind, emotions and psyche must rest and recuperate. So, the stalls are not really stalls. They are rest stops along the way.

But what if a human body is in fine shape and ready to "conquer" the world, and a stall occurs? Well, then, it may very well be, and often is the case, that another human or humans are involved in the process, and they have been stalled for some reason. Hence, the overall slowdown of the train. Often, you can sense the stall is not your own stall. Rather than gnashing your teeth and becoming irritated or anxious that someone is holding up your train—simply focus on other agendas. For if you are living your Soul Ascension Path, you will likely have several, if not many agendas, to which you can attend.

Soul paths or ascension journeys, as mentioned, will have you traipsing here and traveling here and there, but they will always take you to your planned point along the way—eventually. And it is always the right point, because when those points occur, all the stars will have aligned.

WHAT IS ASCENSION?

Before we discuss hierarchy in the Light, we must define for you a term you will see quite frequently in this work, and that is "ascension." If you look at the *Merriam Webster Dictionary* definition of this word, you will see the following: "rising or increasing to higher levels, values, or degrees." This sums up what we mean when we refer to ascension, which is essentially experiencing increasingly greater levels of enlightenment.

You can think of ascension as earning an educational degree—or in this case an endless string of degrees leading to greater and greater enlightenment. When a soul arrives at certain levels of ascension, the soul becomes eligible for a hierarchical master status—which we will now outline.

HIERARCHICAL LEVELS IN THE LIGHT

We present the levels here just to let you know there is a plan, a scheme, a master guidance system.

You will be glad to know that every soul has its own path, but not every soul will want, or be able to ascend to higher levels such as that of Archangels or Seraphim. This is due to the fact that each soul has a one-of-a-kind journey. The spark in each soul has a unique imprint and cannot be replicated. We shall talk more of "sparks" later.

When it comes to ascension, becoming an Archangel is only one possible scenario. You may be thinking you are too late and all the Archangel spots have been taken. It is true that certain ones are occupied, but there are new Archangels entering the Angelic Realm every day and "change" is the fundamental principle inherent in all that occurs on Earth, in the Universe, and even the Multiverse (which is the collectivity comprised of all the Universes in the Cosmos). So even the hierarchy in the Light is not immune to constant change.

Seraphim

Seraphim are the highest order of Angels. They sit at the right hand of the Archangels and are comprised of very high-level energy. In fact, they are made of such high-frequency energy that they are nearly impossible to see with the human eye. If a Seraphim was to visit someone on the EarthPlane, the most the person would see would be very faint sparkles of light.

To become a Seraphim is a very high honor, for these are otherworldly, extremely wise souls capable of imparting the most potent of the Angelic Realm's healing and knowledge.

Archangels

Archangels are of the Seraphim, yet they could best be classified as leaders of the Angels. Each Archangel has specialized skills used for the betterment of the LightPlane and the EarthPlane. There are many Archangels known on the EarthPlane, including the Archangels Michael, Metatron, Gabriel, and Haniel—to name but just a few. Unbeknownst to many humans, there are many other Archangels. This is due to the fact that souls are continuing to ascend to Archangel status. While Archangels do appear on the EarthPlane when called upon by humans, they may not be recognized as Archangels. In such cases, they often take on a human form of some sort.

Becoming an Archangel is a rare occurrence, and not surprisingly, a high honor with equally elevated responsibility. To become an Archangel, one must be a member of the Seraphim Realm for an extended period of time and be studying various forms of healing and communicating. While preparing for Archangel status, a soul identifies specialized skills it possesses and can use for the Higher Good. Often, Archangels spend at least one lifetime on the EarthPlane honing these skills.

Ascended Masters

Ascended Masters are souls who dwell perpetually in the Light, yet visit the EarthPlane often to impart wisdom and knowledge to the mass of humanity. There have been many Ascended Masters on the EarthPlane—for instance Jesus, Buddha, St. Germain, Mother Mary, Afra, Hilarion, and Mother Teresa—to name just a few. The main purpose of being an Ascended Master is to assist souls on the EarthPlane to understand their soul purpose and soul journey.

To become an Ascended Master, one must have lived many human existences in a wide variety of forms so that one can understand the struggles a soul experiences on the EarthPlane at a deep level. While an Ascended Master may return to Earth to teach and enlighten once this status is gained, such a soul generally only does so a limited number of times. Instead, the Ascended Master remains in the Light—teaching and enlightening from the Light via Earthbound souls able to channel and impart the wisdom—as has occurred in the writing of this book.

Elementals

It is lesser known on the EarthPlane that souls can be and are from the Elemental Realm. By this we are referring to those mystical, magical beings many in human form consider "make-believe" or "fantasy." This includes entities such as fairies, elves, sprites, unicorns, mermaids and mermen, and genies. While it seems that this must certainly be something that couldn't be true, we assure you that it is. Of course, these entities don't actually appear as depicted by humans—because they are energetic beings. But they do have their own particular type of energy and way of being.

That being said, there are souls aspiring to become elemental entities. Why would someone want to become a fairy, elf or mermaid? Here we will dispel the notion that these are child's play beings. Instead, these are all very powerful entities with definite soul purposes. Elementals work within realms housed within the Light. For instance, the Fairy Realm is an extension of the Light and that is where fairies reside.

To become an Elemental is no easy task. One must study on the EarthPlane, as well as in the particular realm chosen, and then reside for an extended period of time within that realm while visiting the EarthPlane to offer assistance when called upon. Often assistance is requested by children, who are more likely to see through the Veil to the Other Side and believe in the power of what they see.

Guides, including Life Guides

The task of a Guide is to guide humans while on the Earth-Plane. This means the relationship between a Guide and a human is EarthPlane-based. While a Guide (such as a Life Guide) will certainly commune with a soul in the Light, doing so is primarily to review how a lifetime on the Earth went or to prepare for a new one.

There are many types of guides. The life guide helps lead a soul through the human existence. Generally, a life guide is present for each lifetime a soul decides to reincarnate. That means the life guide agrees to help a soul as long as the soul decides to reincarnate. Not surprisingly, this is a huge commitment and is not taken lightly by either party. There are many other types of guides, including creativity, healing, health, wealth, career, and more.

To become a guide, one must have lived many lifetimes on the EarthPlane so that one can most effectively help guide souls in human form. In addition, a life guide must have lived several lifetimes with the soul they are guiding. It is important that an affinity between the two souls is formed and that they bond.

SOUL ASCENSION PATHS

Just as there are many paths one can take to enlightenment while on the EarthPlane, there are many Soul Ascension Paths within the Light. While we don't have the time or space here to review all the paths, nor would it be of vital significance to you at this time, suffice it to say there are many Soul Ascension Paths, and that they are well-traveled.

One chooses a Soul Ascension Path based on the soul's higher Soul Journey goals. Just as there are many ways to seek education and paths to do so, there are many such ways in the Light.

ORIGINATION AND BREAKING OFF POINT

By the Breaking Off Point we are referring to the point at which your soul breaks free from reincarnating in human form and you no longer return to Earth. This is something that is quite unique to each soul. Therefore, we cannot give you a prescribed level of ascension in these terms. Here, however, is what we can give you in this arena.

1. Each soul is unique in when it chooses to stop coming back to a human form. There is no one set way or timing in which this end occurs for souls.

2. Though there may be no set point as to when reincarnation ceases for all souls, each individual soul plans a breaking off point. This is preordained from the very beginning of a soul's spark. As already mentioned, we shall be covering more about soul sparks later in the book. Suffice it to say for now that a spark is the point when each soul is created or born. Therefore, know that your intention to reincarnate is determined at your beginning—or near your beginning, when you plan out your overall Soul Map. While you have Life Maps for each Earthbound

reincarnation, you also plan an overall Soul Map for your Soul. This Map covers all your plans for ascension. While it contains many set points for your soul, it is a real-time, work-in-progress type of energetic document that has no end.

3. While it is human nature to be curious and strive to discover and find out how many reincarnations you will have on the EarthPlane, we suggest you do not ask this question. Not because it might, as you say, "jinx" you in some way. Merely because the translated answer is likely not to make sense. This is because (as will be covered later in the book), you live many types of lifetimes on the EarthPlane. These include parallel lives and parallel existences, the latter referring to short-term parallel lesson lifetimes located within an alternate human form dimension. (If you are feeling confusion or are overwhelmed at this point, simply take a deep breath and set down the book or reread this paragraph.) This will all come to make more sense the more you read and digest the material. And know that when you sleep, your soul will reiterate the teachings to you via your higher self, and you shall wake up with a great understanding and knowing that seems to have come for "nowhere," and yet it has certainly come from somewhere. It has come from the Light.

THE RIGHT TO CHOOSE (FREE WILL)

Every soul has the right to do as he or she chooses and exercise their free will. In fact, free will is the Law of the Universe. While this may seem as if there are some "buts" to add to this, there truly aren't. While there are constraints souls must live within—at the same time, the soul truly is free to be as the soul wishes to be. To some on the EarthPlane, this may spell a disaster of sorts.

You may feel that if each soul is free and able to do as each soul so chooses, then anarchy will surely reign! The answer to this is yes and no. But it is not as you may envision. For the anarchy lies not with the soul doing what the soul wishes to do. Anarchy ensues when other souls try to control and mediate the actions of other souls. Anarchy is bred from the attempt of souls to stifle and control other souls. But, and there is a big "but" here that needs to be addressed, what if the souls stifling other souls are exerting their own free will and doing as they choose? How, Dear Bhagwan, do you explain that?

While a soul does have the right to do as he or she chooses—that could mean meddling in the life of another in minor things such as expressing opinions, or major things such as keeping that person hostage—if the meddling is in opposition to another's free will, it is not within the acceptable scope of what free will is technically about. However, one is nevertheless exerting one's free will when doing as he or she chooses.

We realize from here in the Light that these concepts are hard for some of you reading this to understand. We are explaining how it is in the Light, while at the same time, we are aware of your context of being on Earth. Therein lies the difficulty with explaining and expressing this information. You are internalizing the information from your position as your Lower Self on Earth and are not in the Light. However, you do have access to the knowledge coming from your higher self, which is that part of you always in the Light. Many are not aware of what their higher self communicates to them, however. That being said, a wide majority of these concepts can seem heretical and preposterous at times.

To say a soul wants to be held captive and suffer while in human form to learn certain lessons may sound absurd. Yet that is what does occur. It is therefore within reason that a person exerted free will and in fact asked to be held hostage, or to have cancer, or to be in a job that is going nowhere, or a relationship that is not working well. The list goes on. You exerted your free will to learn lessons, and the only way you could learn some of these lessons was for another soul to step in and impede your progress in one way or another.

Of course, the seeming opposite to this does occur also, but the results are the same. By that we are saying you also call forth souls who will help you along your journey of learning lessons. These individuals will seem to be and are "on your side" on the EarthPlane. And they do assist rather than impede you. But the bottom line is this. Those souls assisting aren't doing anything differently than those impeding you. All the efforts—from both sides—are teaching you valuable lessons you had asked to learn.

DO SOULS MISBEHAVE IN THE LIGHT?

Yes and no. If we are to consider misbehaving as stepping out of line in terms of not agreeing with other souls, then yes, they do misbehave. But as was mentioned in the previous section, free will is the law of the Universe. That means that free will trumps all, and free will allows you to do as you choose. Within reason, of course, and within certain parameters. For yes, though it may sound as if it is a sort of "Wild West" in the Light, there are certain principles and rules that must be abided by, and certain actions that a soul would not, and even could not, take.

WHAT ARE THE "RULES" IN THE LIGHT?

Ah, this is quite an important question. Are there any rules? To answer the question—yes, there are rules in the Light. However, the rules don't look like rules on the EarthPlane. Let me explain.

Rules are the by-products of living a human existence and they are more constricted and rigid than rules in the Light. It is very important that rules are assigned and adhered to, even in the Light. However, this is not for the same reasons they are designed and enforced on the Earth.

Rules are instituted in the Light to guide and to empower.

This ensures that souls stay on course and receive vital information as they maintain those courses, and even change those courses.

Rules in the Light are more about helping souls advance than they are about controlling them. Many of the rules on the Earth-Plane are created to keep souls in line—to ensure they don't step out of line and onto the toes or feet or whole body of another. Rules are significant and important on the EarthPlane, yet they are not the same as in the Light.

So, what more should you know about rules in and out of the Light? Here is more information about those rules.

A. Rules are meant to be broken in the Light, as they are sometimes meant to be broken on the EarthPlane. Often the breaking of the rules is a means by which an individual is exerting his or her free will.
B. Rules are meant to guide more so in the Light than they are on the EarthPlane, but still, they are a guidance system, even for souls in human form.
C. Rules are most definitely necessary on the EarthPlane and in the Light. Truly, an organized society— whether of the Light or of the Earth—requires guidelines. Lines within which to color. And even if an individual on the Earth or a soul in the Light decides to color outside of the lines—it was those lines that were originally responsible.

CONSEQUENCES OF "MISBEHAVING" IN THE LIGHT

While it may be surprising, misbehaving does occur in the Light, and there are consequences souls face when this occurs. While it isn't a penalty as you have on the EarthPlane, nonetheless, there is a type of cessation of ideas. A soul who steps out of line and into the "Light Lane" of another will be stopped from

JULIE BAWDEN-DAVIS & BHAGWAN SHREE RAJNEESH

furthering ideas along the lines of what started their stepping out of line.

As has been said here, free will is the Law of the Universe. Therefore, any misbehaving in the Light occurs when actions impinge upon another soul's free will. It may seem surprising that this is even able to happen or possible to happen in the Light. For the vision that you humans have of the Light is perfection. And to you, most definitely, perfection would mean that nothing "bad" or out of order ever happens in the Light and all goes according to plan. Herein lies the issue with that thought process. According to plan. According to whose plan? All souls in the Light have free will—therefore all souls in the Light have their own plans. You can see where this is going, can't you?

So, yes, at times souls do step out of line—step out of their lane—and they step into another's lane, and they impinge on free will, if even for a nanosecond. And when they do this, they are considered as "misbehaving." All thoughts that brought on the sidestepping into another's path are required to be expunged from their soul path and the soul path of the other, so that all may be "righted" in the Universe and even in the Multiverse.

Now I hear you thinking, is that all? No exile to a type of purgatory? I'm afraid it is much less dramatic than that. The thoughts that brought the soul to step into another's path are no longer allowed. The expunging process is the consequence. And no, that process doesn't cause pain and it isn't dramatic. It is a simple extraction, with no "warning" to not repeat the same, because a warning isn't necessary. The extraction removes the thought process that led to the stepping out of line in the first place.

THE COLLECTIVE CONSCIOUSNESS HAS THE FINAL SAY

Not surprisingly, the collective consciousness—that collection of all souls in the Light—has the final say when it comes to what can and can't be done and what should and shouldn't be undone.

When a soul "steps out of line," the collective consciousness —the Oneness of "We"—does determine if free will has been trodden upon and what should be done about the fact. By what should be done, we refer to how far back in the consciousness of what occurred will the erasure occur. If you are surmising from this statement that we are suggesting actions are rewound and rewritten in the Light, you would be right.

We know this will not sit well with many on the EarthPlane, for going back in time and righting seeming "wrongs" is only something that happens in time-travel fiction. Yet that is how these items are taken care of in the Light.

If you wish to "sit with this" for some time, we encourage you to do so. For this is heady stuff, and not something that you can absorb in an afternoon. As you have seen, the LightPlane is very different from the EarthPlane in many ways—yet in some ways it is the same. At this juncture in this volume of work, we are discussing how the LightPlane is dissimilar. However, we have touched on some similarities. One significant similarity is the presence of free will and its power. For free will on the EarthPlane is the answer to the age-old question, "Why do bad things happen?" And it is also the answer to the less-asked question, "Why do good things happen?"

As you digest this book, we suggest you bite off as much as you can chew, and that you chew it for some time, until what you have read resonates with what you have come to understand about the Light. And then you may, if you choose, continue reading and digesting and assimilating further "facts" about the LightPlane and its relation to the EarthPlane, and to the Universe and the Multiverse (which is all the universes collectively).

A few more final thoughts about the role of the "collective consciousness." This is an overwhelming topic that many have tried to wrangle with and understand. While we cannot tell you everything there is to know about it at this point, we can tell you there is a collective consciousness, and that it is quite powerful. In fact, the collective consciousness has a great deal to do with what happens, what will happen, and what does not happen in the Light.

We know the idea of a collective consciousness can seem confusing. You may be thinking and wondering that if there is a collective consciousness, how does "free will" fit into this paradigm? And which has priority—the collective consciousness or individual free will? Not surprisingly, this is not easily answered. As you are probably noticing, there are many nuances when it comes to what occurs in the Light. There are some things, however, we can tell you to help make this clearer.

Free will does trump all. And that is free will of the individual. However, the LightPlane does run in a sort of democratic style— for lack of a better term. With this, we are referring to those "global" decisions and issues that require solving. When there is something to solve, those individual souls with a stake in the issue and outcome come forth. When they come forth, they express their opinions. You may be thinking the opinions are likely to be wildly divergent. To this we will say, yes and no. We take into account that those interested in a particular issue will tend to be thinking along the same lines. That being said, there is often an ability to compromise and talk through an issue to come to a mutually agreed-upon solution that often all souls agree upon.

However, when this doesn't happen, there is a process that we go through. It is again a democratic process. It is a sort of blending of the minds that results in a compromise. We in fact blend all our thoughts, as if into a giant blender, and then the answers come forth. This is a very simplistic way of explaining this concept. But suffice it to say, we "do" come up with a solution. For in the Light, questions and conflicts, as they are, never linger. They are dealt with as rapidly and as effectively as possible. There is a reason for this. And that is that energetically it does not work to have unresolved issues floating about. Rather, we must resolve all loose ends as soon as they become loose. If that were not to occur, the symbiosis that has existed in the Light since the beginning of time would not prevail.

However, it is impossible that it wouldn't prevail, for as has been said on the EarthPlane, and I can attest to now, the Light Force is the most powerful in the Multiverse.

This brings up questions. Namely, how do situations and events occur on the EarthPlane that seem contrary to the Light? Such as war and famine, for instance. Once again, we return to free will. In this instance, the free will to learn as a human what cannot be learned as a being of the Light.

ARE SOULS EVER LOST?

This is a question to which many on the EarthPlane wish to know the answer. And I am here to answer this question for you. Firstly, however, I would like you to ask yourself this question. If you were to do something untoward that did not better humankind or reflect well on you in the Light, would you like to be erased? We presume, since you are reading this, that the answer would most likely be "no." You would want a chance or even several chances, to redeem yourself.

We must first define "lost" before we can discuss if souls ever reach this state. For the purposes of this book, we shall refer to "lost" as souls that simply disappear. This is not to be confused with souls that make a misstep and face the consequences of doing so—from a LightPlane perspective, as mentioned in the previous section on "misbehaving," and from a soul growth purpose perspective. We will explain the latter concept further in a moment.

And now to answer the question whether souls ever disappear. They do not. Once a soul is established, a soul is eternal, wherever that soul may find itself. So, the idea of a soul simply vanishing is something that does not occur in the Universe or even in the Multiverse. In the human sense, there is no "ashes to ashes" or "dust to dust." There is only universal eternity.

Now to address the idea that a soul may make a misstep and face the consequences. This most certainly can and does occur when souls walk out of their LightPlane lanes. When this happens, lessons are learned. As a result of missteps, souls become more enlightened and the soul expansion journey continues—any "missteps" immediately forgotten.

SOUL DNA MIND MAP/LIFE MAP

We are including the definitions of the following concepts here, as understanding these terms will further enhance your comprehension as you read. (For the definition of more terms, see the Glossary at the end of the book.)

Life Map: A map of your journey on Earth for a reincarnation.

Mind Map: The view or map of a "soul's journey" as it is imprinted in that soul's mind. The mind map changes over time in some respects, but in many respects it stays the same from lifetime to lifetime.

Soul Journey: This refers to the journey, which is neverending, of a soul. It is the mapping of the soul's complete and often complex journey from the soul spark stage and onwards. Each human lifetime is included in this soul journey, as well as all the other learning and "ascension pinpoints" along the way.

RELEVANCE OF THE IDEA OF "ONENESS"

If you take a look at many of the writings and teachings of modern day "gurus" and such, you will see that the idea of oneness is emphasized. In a way, the idea of oneness is correct, but in another way, it is truly about oneness of self, rather than oneness of all. By that I mean that while we are all souls on divine journeys, and we have similarities, we are truly our own souls. So, in that sense, the idea that we are "all one" is inaccurate. Otherwise, how could there be individual free will, if this was so? And would we truly want "oneness" of all, anyway?

Yes, we are all of like mind and like soul and like body when in the human form, but no—we are not "as one." From the Light-Plane perspective, the idea of being "as one" is that if you hurt one, you do harm to all. Not because we are all one soul, but rather because the energetic frequency that is begotten by harming one does reverberate and cause harm to all.

I can see you scratching your head, and that is not surprising. This is a heady topic. Perhaps the headiest of topics in all we shall discuss here. Or at least one of the headiest.

While we don't wish to confuse or muddy the issue, we do wish to try to clear up some of the confusion surrounding this idea. You may have noticed in history on the EarthPlane, there are times when humans have tried to live as one in a communal state. In fact, I did just that in my last incarnation as Bhagwan, and in many ways, I made quite a stir. However, the idea of oneness, and the push and pull required to achieve such oneness, just doesn't work in the human existence. While many of the ideals are quite honorable, and often start out with good intentions, they soon slip and slide, as if down a muddy cliff in a rainstorm, until many of those ideals have fallen by the proverbial wayside.

But why, if souls are enlightened (as those of you reading this book are), cannot humans come together as one and create an understanding and a communion of oneness in terms of a way of life? A way of life without strife and struggle and jealousy and hatred and violence? If you cast your mind back several pages to the main law of the Universe—free will—then you have won the "prize" here. As mentioned, free will trumps all, and free will takes precedence over humans' fleeting desire to be and think and act as one. For in the end, truly, all souls wish to be free. Free to roam as they choose, and free to think and act as they choose. This is counterintuitive and at cross purposes with the idea of oneness. So, although it is a "nice" thought, as you say—it is just that.

WHAT OF THE "TWIN FLAME" CONNECTION AND JOURNEY?

Here we shall also comment on a fairly new phenomenon known as the "twin flame" connection and journey. The idea is that there are two souls who are essentially one. The "story" goes that these two souls split at some point. This has resulted in their missing their other half until they find one another and unite once again as one while on the EarthPlane.

If you read the prior information in this book about souls being a single being, and the idea of free will, you can see that this idea of a twin flame is essentially impossible, and to be frank, preposterous. Additionally, would you truly wish to be a half of a whole soul that requires union with the other half to be whole? If you look at this from a logical perspective, as you say on Earth, it is quite impossible. How would free will be possible if there are two souls, both of whom are likely, at least part of the time, to be pushing and pulling in different directions?

Where this phenomenon of twin flames and sentiments such as "you complete me" stem from is the common desire of humans to merge with one another. This longing to merge with another, however, signifies a loss of connection between the human lower self and the higher self/soul. A yearning to merge with another human is truly a disguised wish to merge with one's higher self and soul. When there is a lack in the human lower self, it is truly because one is cut off from the Oneness of Self we mentioned in the previous section. If one can merge one's lower and higher selves while in human form as much as possible, one will feel whole and have no need to try to fill a hole with another soul. The fact is, it is impossible to fill a hole with another soul, for we are all meant to be whole on our own while in human form, and we are always whole in the Light.

As mentioned, however, this wanting and seeming need to merge with another is quite common for those in human form. That being said, this overriding desire does cause people to invent phenomena such as twin flames and the notion of needing another person to complete oneself. For this then gives a "valid" reason for wanting and yearning to merge with another soul. At the same time, all of this offers abundant learning lessons for a soul while in human form, as those learning lessons lead to soul expansion.

WHAT OF SOULMATES?

This latter discussion brings up the notion of soulmates, to which we shall say they are indeed "a thing." In fact, many who believe they have joined with a "twin flame," have actually reunited with a soulmate. We are referring to two souls who align in and out of the Light. In the alignment, lessons are learned and often great accomplishments are achieved. At the same time, such souls find joy and comfort in the connection with one another. The concept of soulmates is also far reaching. It refers to romantic partnerships, as well as many other types of close unions, including friendships and parent/sibling relationships. (We cover the topic of soulmates to a greater extent in Part Three.)

SOUL PURPOSE AND ITS CONNECTION WITH THE DIVINE

Being at one with self is not to say that one's soul purpose has no connection with the Divine, and that one is merely on one's own. On the contrary, the Divine—we are referring to the community in the Light and the LightPlane overall—is very much intertwined with one's soul purpose. For one's soul purpose is born in and of the Divine.

Let us explain.

Our souls sparked (originated) in the Divine. Our very way of being does and did spring forth from the Divine. Therefore, it is as much a part of us as any other dimension. In fact, more so. For as mentioned, we are born in and of the Divine Light.

Why is this of significance?

The Divine or The Light or the Other Side or Beyond the Veil (however you wish to refer to it) is other-worldly compared to the EarthPlane. The Divine is the essence of the soul. It is where the soul resides—always. The soul does not leave the Divine—ever.

With this in mind, we can see that the Divine is the most important place, and yet, of course, it is not the only place. There are many other dimensions—the EarthPlane being one of them. But the Divine, i.e. the Light, is where all higher order thinking and being takes place. And so, it is the place where it all begins— even more than soul sparks—although they are essential to the entire order of things. The Light is the epicenter of the Cosmos or the Multiverse. There are other realms where very high-level thinking takes place. Yet, the Light does transcend those locations, because of two key elements—that of certain higher-level emotions and thoughts. Much like the EarthPlane, the Light contains feelings and intellect. While this doesn't seem readily apparent in the Light, if you listen to recollections from those who have had near-death experiences, they often say they experienced an overriding feeling of peace and a sort of "all-knowing" when they momentarily slipped into the Light.

While the Divine is the most important place and where the soul resides, the EarthPlane can be considered as a giant board game. This is where you go to "play out" your existence on the EarthPlane so that you can learn certain soul-expanding lessons. With this analogy, you can see that reality is in the Light, while make-believe is on Earth.

We know this is very hard to digest at times. For on the Earth-Plane, you are living in what seems like a "hard, harsh reality." The very Earth itself is quite solid. So, we suggest you read in bite-sized portions—especially when you feel a bit overwhelmed by the content we are laying out in front of you. In fact, that is how the channeling of this information also occurred. In bite-sized pieces. One page at a time with rest and digestion and assimilation in between.

The Divine is where the "essences" of each of our souls lies—as if enshrined. One's essences are an "enormous" part of the soul. While the soul itself is indestructible and all powerful, essences can be likened to a baby in the womb—they are quite fragile. The Light—with its many protections—is the best and only place for one's essences to reside. We shall speak again about our essences later in the book and how they relate to our inception as a spark.

Where to Go from Here?

We will pause at this point to give you a breather in your reading and to ask this question. Where should you "take" this information? For it is, as mentioned, quite heady, and at the same time, quite revealing. No doubt, you have already had many questions answered. If this has occurred, we commend you for your absorption of the material, and even more importantly, for your higher-level understanding of it. For this information is not something that everyone can hear or understand, and certainly not many will be able to assimilate. That is not to make us or (even you) sound "highbrow or exceptional." It is only to explain why you may share this work with another—even another whom you see as ascended—and it will not resonate as deeply as with you. Or it could resonate even more deeply.

Now that we have finished with these qualifications regarding acceptance by others of our "truths," we will delve into deeper topics that will be of interest and assistance to you at this time on the EarthPlane.

WHY AND HOW CERTAIN SOULS "ALIGN" WITH ONE ANOTHER

It is interesting to note that certain souls align with one another in the Light, as they do on the EarthPlane. In some respects, this seems to be counterintuitive to what humans would expect to be the case, given the "oneness" idea. However, as was pointed out prior to our discussion of oneness as a myth, we are all souls with similarities at one level. But we are also blessed with free will—and those elements of free will may cause us to reach out and unite with certain other souls—but not every soul.

This raises the "awkward" question of whether certain souls dislike each other in the Light as they dislike each other on the EarthPlane. The short answer is yes and no. The long answer is quite long, but we shall attempt to explain it to you briefly.

The idea of "disliking" is an enigma in the Light. This feeling is toned down quite a bit in the Light and looks very little like the dislike you know so well on the EarthPlane. You would not recognize it as such in the Light. Therefore, you may be wondering—does it matter? Is this something that should even be discussed?

Once again, yes and no. Yes, dislike should be discussed, because it is a construct of the EarthPlane—a quite powerful one that has its impact. Dislike is generally the precursor to hate, and those who are on the EarthPlane and or have ever been there, know where hate leads. To confusion and destruction and anger, which can lead to further outcomes such as war, famine, homelessness, disease, and pestilence—to name but a few.

WHAT IS DISLIKE, THEN, IN THE LIGHT?

We will describe dislike in the Light as a sort of mild repulsion—where one soul will shy away from the energy of the other soul, and in some instances both are repelled, like the opposite ends of a magnet on the EarthPlane. For, as has been mentioned, the Light is completely composed of energy. Sensations, thoughts and emotions, while also energy, are human energetic responses, and are not of the Light. Therefore, in the Light you could say we don't have a translation system for baser human emotions such as dislike.

Yes, we hear your human brain striving to analyze these concepts and to put them in the "right" order in your mind. We do urge you once again to remember we are not truly comparing apples with apples here, as you say, given that the very nature of the Light is so different than the EarthPlane.

We are doing our best to give you a glimpse or a bird's-eye-view into the LightPlane realm in such a way that you can digest and understand what you are reading. Will there be "misunderstandings" of this information at times? Yes, of course. We suggest that whenever a concept is not easily understood at first, you give your mind a rest and come back and read the passage in question again at a later time when it is comfortable for you to do so. At some point, its meaning will become clearer to you. If it doesn't today, it may very well do so tomorrow, or in a week, month, year, decade, or dare we say—a lifetime from now.

DOES ANYONE IN PARTICULAR HAVE A "FINAL SAY" HERE ON THE OTHER SIDE?

If so, who?

This is a valid question for humans to ask regarding the Light, for on Earth there needs to be individuals with the final say, or else anarchy on the EarthPlane would surely reign. And given the human proclivity to want to outdo and outrank one another, it would be a rather "messy" proposition to not have those individuals in place who have the final say.

However, in the Light, matters are quite different. In fact, if it were not for each soul's need to continue to ascend, no hierarchy would be necessary. Yet, in that case, there would be no need for the Earth, as well. For souls do leave the comfort and safety of the Light for the "hard knock" lessons the EarthPlane does provide.

Regarding whom has final say in the Light, we do know on the EarthPlane there is an idea of God, Allah, Buddha, and such beings reigning from the Light. While we are not going to dispute that such beings exist, we will say the all-powerful influence given to these various deities is a bit overrated. For, as mentioned, there is free will for all. And at the same time, there is a hierarchy. That being said, there is no one being capable of refuting the aspirations of others. There may be consequences for actions deemed as veering out of one's lane, as mentioned, but no all-powerful being who usurps others, exists. We do know this is a bit on the confusing side, and we do hope that this makes sense to you—at least at some level.

HOW YOU CLIMB THE HIERARCHICAL LADDER OF POWER IN THE LIGHT

First, we must discuss the definition of the Ladder of Power. Once again, this is not easily compared to a ladder of power on the EarthPlane. For on the EarthPlane, such a ladder would be headed up by the most powerful—the one who can squelch and even abolish the wishes, desires, and intent of others. As just mentioned, such an all-powerful being does not exist within the LightPlane. There is no rejecting occurring in the Light. There may be a type of sidestepping for those souls who don't align with the plans of another soul, but there is simply no pushing down, overpowering, or overrunning. There is no, "this is better than that," or "I am better than you" in the Light.

While this does sound like welcome words to many who have been pushed down while on the EarthPlane, at the same time it causes a bit of unease amongst those who have climbed the hierarchical EarthPlane ladder and "made something of themselves" at the expense of others. That being said, the "dog-eat-dog" of the EarthPlane does not exist in the Light.

The question now undoubtedly arising in your mind is how does one advance on a Ladder of Power if there is no power over which to overcome? You might be thinking that certainly anarchy would reign supreme in such a context.

The BIG difference here—the game changer, as you would say —is that the Power Ladder is an "inside job." One must out best and even wrestle with and overpower oneself to climb the ladder. And yes, you guessed it, every person has his or her own ladder. No two ladders are the same.

This last statement will bewilder or even downright annoy some of you Earth beings. For it may seem that the sentiment flies in the face of community and discounts it. Are we saying that each man, woman, and child is an island? Yes and no. Yes, all souls are meant to be their "own persons," yet each soul does not operate in a vacuum. For souls to exist and coexist, there must be other souls with whom to do so.

So how does this present us with a quandary, you might ask? And what is that quandary? We shall show it to you in the form of an equation, which will assist you in digesting what we are relating.

Male+female=union=child
Male+female or being+being=strife (when the two are at odds)
Being+being=great ideas and wisdom (when the two are in sync)

So, how does this fit into the scheme of things—this I/we/us against or at odds with the world or in sync with the world?

The journey, any journey, will always be fraught with strife and challenges and mountains, as you say, to overcome and climb over, or even shovel through. This is the same on the EarthPlane, as it is in the Light. We know that some of you reading this are doing a bit of head scratching at this point and wondering, isn't the Light supposed to be "smooth sailing?" Once again, yes and no. Yes, it is smooth sailing in that you will get to where you wish to go in Divine time, but no, you won't always meet with an unhindered journey.

But?!

How?!

I thought?!

We can hear you saying this and much more. Meaning, we know you think the Light is, shall we say, all peaches and cream or however you wish to describe an "easy ride." Isn't the Light supposed to be the exact opposite of the EarthPlane? So much easier and freeing, and just plain fun?!?

Again, yes and no.

While there are no physical hindrances in the Light, there are Soul expansion hindrances. For if there weren't, what would be the purpose of striving? Oh, this sounds so, so, so, human, you may be thinking!

We will only say to that, "sort of." By that we are referring to the following "facts."

1. The experience in the Light is not human, because it is not a physical experience. This is the "biggest" difference between the LightPlane and the EarthPlane. There truly is no physical pain in the Light, for there is no physical body as you know it on the EarthPlane.

2. At the same time, there is a sort of pain of the psyche, but not pain so much as discomfort. This can occur as your soul attempts to strive to move forward— sometimes when it isn't time.

But, but, but! We hear you saying. Isn't the LightPlane perfect compared to the EarthPlane? Doesn't everything run smoothly and perfectly there? We will answer once again, sort of.

We hear you sighing so loudly at this point, as this all seems quite confusing, and yet it isn't. Because your soul does understand and even like this ever so confusing concept. Let us explain what we mean by that.

SOUL EXPANSION PLANS CHANGE

In the Light, one's plans for soul expansion are not set in stone as you may be thinking they certainly must be from your human existence perspective. The belief on Earth is that the LightPlane existence is perfection. But we must remind you that perfection is a human term. (Yes, I know I was a human at one point—as were all of us involved in imparting these words of wisdom here, or we wouldn't be assigned this task.) The idea of perfection was constructed so that humans would feel as if there exists a place within the Universe where there is no strife, torment, dejection, or severe loss, as the EarthPlane so readily serves up on a regular basis.

While the Light certainly does offer a wonderful place of solace and peace without the human experience of strife, the Light does not offer up a "get out of jail free" experience, so to speak. You are accountable in the Light. Accountable to others? Certainly, as you must co-exist, but more importantly, accountable to yourself. That being said, as you make your way along your Soul Ascension Path toward your own "personal best," you require the ability to adapt and be flexible, because your goals and aspirations as a soul will change as you ascend.

But, but, but, we hear you saying again, isn't everything laid out in terms of a soul's expansion? Isn't everything figured out ahead of time and for eternity? That is once again another concept devised by humans to understand what is occurring with your soul. Yes, everything is devised ahead of time for each of your EarthPlane reincarnations, but your overall, enduring soul journey is certainly not set in stone. You wouldn't want it to be, would you?

This is the point where we must unstick the EarthPlane existence from one's LightPlane existence. We realize this is not an easy task, but how else can you understand what is occurring on the EarthPlane and in the Light if you don't have a framework in which to understand it? Well, this is what this book is all about! Dismantling common frameworks so that you can see the inner workings, and then putting them back together in a manner that answers questions and tends to bolster the soul while doing so. For further exploration of this topic, let's look at the following concepts regarding the relationship between the EarthPlane and the LightPlane.

THE "GAME" OF LIFE

While the EarthPlane existence is quite naturally a part of the LightPlane existence, the LightPlane existence is not as much a part of the EarthPlane existence.

If you look closely at what we've just said, you will see we are inferring that the EarthPlane is indeed a fabricated way of being that is not real in the "real" sense. It has been devised so you can learn lessons. Much like a board game is created and constructed so that you can play and learn how to maneuver yourself within the rules of the game. That is what the EarthPlane is. A giant "Game of Life."

Some are aghast at the idea of the EarthPlane being a game. For life is so serious!! Very important things are occurring on Earth that people need to take notice of!! News stations drone on all day announcing important, vital, earthshattering occurrences that people must get up in arms about, or the unthinkable might happen!

We, of course, chuckle at some of the dire warnings pronounced from the EarthPlane. The word "unthinkable" being one of those words that does muster up great worry and fear amongst humans. The irony is the unthinkable is what you call death, and what we call being "in and of the Light." Therefore, your unthinkable is our natural way of being. Of course, this doesn't take into consideration those people—loved ones—you leave behind when the unthinkable does happen and you return to the Light.

There is a philosophy of thought created by man known as Stoicism, which dates back centuries, but the concepts of this way of living and being while on the EarthPlane are quite universal. From our perspective in the Light, some Stoicism concepts describe the ideal way to traverse one's EarthPlane existence.

One such concept says there is no point in focusing on what isn't currently there within your EarthPlane existence, even though you wish and pray those things were there. This could be more money or a grander home or a significant other. Rather, the idea is not to consider these items as anything, for they aren't at this time. So, ignore what you do not have but want.

While this flies in the face of some schools of thought on manifestation, we in the Light suggest living this way, for it is the most peaceful way of existing. This is what you call "living in the now." For as stoicism points out, focusing on the past and what you didn't do but wish you did will only keep you regretful and unhappy. You cannot do anything about the past, which is truly gone—at least in the touch, taste, feel way of the human existence. The past can reside in your mind, of course, and visiting the past can help instill vital learning lessons, but doing anything else with the memories is not a healthy way to live on the EarthPlane. Focusing on the past invites melancholy and despair.

Worrying about what might happen in the future is also not of value. The truth is that human worries tend to outshine true reality. This occurs because the human mind is quite good at making up and sharing dire potentialities with itself and others. The what ifs will truly what if you into an early "grave," so to speak. You can truly worry yourself to death, or at least worry yourself into a stress-induced existence.

Pull yourself back to the now when you find yourself stuck in such a worrisome loop in the future. Do glance at the future in terms of your dreams, desires, and goals and how you might reach them. But then return to the present. Because staying in a forward-thinking mindset will quickly morph from aspirational to situational. Meaning you will begin to dream up situations you wish would occur, until those situations turn into expectations. Then, as the next week or month or year dawns and those desired situations don't occur, you will become angry and disillusioned and downright snarly and nasty. We suggest skipping this journey to nowhere good and staying in the "real" place of now—with a nod to the past and a glance—just a glance—into the future.

We are at this juncture at the end of this first section of the book. At this point, we will sum up some of what has been said—

the "higher" points, if you will. And then we will move on to the landscape of the Other Side—what it is like to be here.

You have no doubt noticed that while there are many differences between the Light and the EarthPlane, there are a striking number of similarities. Some of them may have surprised you, while some may seem to be the way things would likely be. The overarching, most critical component for you to absorb is that while the journey of the single soul is a solo journey, it is also a collective consciousness journey.

However, and this is a big however, the solo journey of the soul always "win out." Each soul's journey is of the utmost importance to that particular soul. This is not to say that souls can't "come together" to break the proverbial bread and align and ascend and accomplish great things together, but in the end, it is the solo journey of all respective souls that makes up the Light-Plane existence. The solo soul journey is also the goal while one is on the EarthPlane. Souls do come together to accomplish great things on the EarthPlane—and sometimes to destroy things. But in the end, a soul enters the world and leaves the world alone. This is not to sound doomsday; it is just the way it is. Those souls able to accept and assimilate this fact find the soul journey to be soul expanding. This lesson, however, is a very difficult one when in human form. More on how to handle this in the third and final section of the book.

The Landscape on the Other Side

PART TWO

How or what the Other Side looks like is of course a topic of great popularity for humans. And for good reason, as the human experience is a tactile one, and therefore you wish to see, feel, hear, and know what the experience here is like. As you can imagine, or possibly already intuited, it is much different here.

That is not to say that we can't describe what it is like here in a way that you can visualize and understand and makes sense to you. But you will have to extend your imagination, and you should be good at doing that by now—after reading this book!

So, let's get into the landscape of the Other Side, shall we? We will start with the overall feeling or "vibe" here, which may be different than you imagine. On the other hand, you will know and feel and remember that this is how it really is. For you have been here many times before. This is truly your home. We will now explain to you some creature comforts of that home.

HOW IT FEELS ON THE OTHER SIDE

What is the difference between how you would feel if you were to visit the Other Side in human form and how you would feel if you were living there in soul form? And how would it appear to you visually? In both cases, it will be vastly different and it will not be easy for you to understand how a soul would feel—as yet. So, we will begin with your human experience, as that will affect your experience and interpretation of soul and "light" forms.

For example, you might walk down the street on the Other Side, though we don't really have streets. They are more like superhighways. As you walk, you will feel as if you are on a long journey, yet in reality, it is very short. In the blink of a human eye, you will arrive at your destination, however long that journey may be. Nevertheless, you will feel you have been on a long journey. This may be difficult for you to understand at first.

JOURNEY OF DISCOVERY

Being in the Light—on the Other Side—is all about self-discovery and discovery of the Universe. There are very few moments you would consider "wasted" on the LightPlane. Therefore, when you choose to journey to a place within the Light, it is an exercise in self-discovery and learning. It is like putting on an educational audiobook before you set out, which contains the information that enters your brain, psyche, and very being.

You may think this sounds quite marvelous and highly educational—and it is. On the other hand, if you are in human form, it would be overwhelming, and taxing on the human psyche and body. For that reason, it is certainly not a way of being that could work for the human form and mind. Yet, humans try to emulate this way of being when they travel. Hence, the wearing of headphones with audiobooks when they are "working out" or exercising, and even driving their cars.

After a time, however, you will find that you tire of the dual focus inherent in these actions. But this is not a problem when you are in the Light. For then, you can readily absorb at the same time, what can only be described as Light Years of information—and much more complex material.

Do not worry if the idea sounds exhausting. Your soul is able to readily absorb all of the information that it chooses or is programmed to absorb.

DOES THE SOUL EVER BECOME TIRED?

It is generally recognized that there is no illness or disease here in the Light, but you may be wondering as you read, how your soul does absorb such an abundance of information all at once, and if the soul does tire. Our answer to the question, does the soul ever tire, is both yes and no.

Yes, the soul does have pauses in information absorption, and energy can ebb and flow, but the soul does not have the typical human response of, "I am utterly exhausted and must rest my body and mind, so my soul or psyche can perform another function, or absorb more knowledge."

This brings up the idea of resting in the Light. Where do you go to rest? For on the EarthPlane you have your resting places, including beds, cots, hammocks, and the like. We can hear you wondering very urgently where we sleep or rest, and if we do in fact rest at all. We do rest and will now describe the various places in the Light where we do so, and the type of rest that is required.

PLACES TO REST

The Incubator Pod

In the Light, we have an incubator of a sort that helps the soul have a deeper rest than "normal." This ensures a type of rejuvenation and renewal. Incubators are often used when a soul returns from a lifetime on the EarthPlane. As you might suspect, a soul may be a bit bedraggled after such an experience, especially if the EarthPlane existence was particularly demanding.

The best way to describe an incubator to those on the Earth-

Plane is to say that it is like a powdery, fluffy cloud, or pod. And that is how it feels—light and fluffy and nurturing and cuddly and comfortable.

What Occurs in the Pod

Healing occurs at the soul level in the pod, which could never be explained in human terms. When the healing has taken place, everything is "made right again" and the soul is now set on the "right" course. One comes out of the incubator pod feeling completely refreshed and nourished, in such a way that we can only say that absolutely everything feels as if it is in the right order and that nothing is amiss or missing.

The soul's "energetic frequency" is heightened to such a point that if we were to turn that frequency into sound, you would not be able to hear it. In fact, even creatures on the EarthPlane known to hear high frequencies (such as whales and dolphins in the ocean and dogs) would not be able to hear this frequency.

Souls are made of "frequencies," and the higher the frequency that can be heard, the higher the soul is within the ascension process. Therefore, as a soul ascends, these higher frequencies become the norm for the soul's energetic way of being. It is with these higher frequencies that a soul learns what a soul had meant to and means to learn. And it is upon these frequencies that a soul continues the ascension process.

It is important to understand that the pod is a "treat," as you say on the EarthPlane, or even more accurately—a perk. The incubator pod is not something one enters that often. Rather, it is something one does when necessary, and sometimes it is some-thing for which one must "wait." Yes, there is waiting here in the Light! We can hear you sighing, because you probably thought that one of the perks of dying, i.e. slipping sideways, would be to never wait in line again!

THE LIBRARY

There is a sort of resting and learning experience in the Library. We are referring to a library location where you soak up information while your soul is in a state of semi-rest. We know you are thinking this does not seem restful at all—learning while resting. But for the advanced souls of the Universe, of which you are a part, given that you deemed it important to read this tome—this is what happens when you are in the Light. And you did ask how we rest, did you not? You may be wondering if this is the Akashic Records Library? We will refer to the Library as the Great Library in the Sky. The Akashic Records Library is a wing of the Great Library.

What Happens in the Library and Why Go There?

Obviously, learning and soul advancement are a big part of the Library. At the same time, rest occurs. How does this happen? We remind you once again that it is necessary to suspend your imagination when thinking about what it is like in the Light. While it is certainly human for you to try to make a comparison with the EarthPlane, doing so doesn't always work well in this case. What we can say, however, is that when one learns in the Light in what you would consider a resting state, the soul feels rested and is in fact recharged while education occurs.

It is worth repeating that it is very different in the Light compared to the EarthPlane. We are doing our best to express these concepts in ways that you can understand, but it is definitely not comparing apples to apples, as you say. Those who have found it laborious and difficult to learn in school on the EarthPlane will not think of learning as restful, but we assure you that your soul does find great comfort and rest, even while learning. However, it is not about the volume of what is being learned. It is about the subject matter of what is being learned. For example, if you were to learn something on the EarthPlane that offers you great comfort or excitement and a feeling of adventure, how long it took to learn the material is not of much significance. What is of significance is what you learned. What you learned gives you the restful and reenergizing experience.

One learns to be a teacher in the Library, so learning in the Light centers around learning to teach. Why is this important? Because in the hierarchy portion of Part One, we mentioned that some of you are, or will be, studying to be Ascended Masters. Hence the learning in the library in the Light while at rest.

Suffice it to say that in the Light learning is critical to rejuvenation. This is similar to resting while on the EarthPlane, at which time you rejuvenate cells and electrons in the physical body, as well as recharge the muscular system and the organs. This is the closest we can get you to understanding how resting and rejuvenation occurs in the Light and is closely tied to learning. Think of it as a powerful energy source into which you plug your soul. As it does so, it rejuvenates and educates. Quite a "handy" arrangement!

While in the Library during rest, your soul absorbs "essences." Here is another interesting bit of information for you to attempt to absorb. On the EarthPlane, you think of essences as the essential elements of something that are wrapped into a microscopic package. In the Light, essences take on a much more vital role. For essences are truly pieces of your soul—fragments needed to continue to map out a soul's progress and contribute to the growth of the soul. This is quite a heady statement and is not an easy one to understand in human terms. Suffice it to say that while you are in the Library resting, you are absorbing essences— of oneself and only oneself.

THE MEADOW

The Meadow is a resting place which can be most closely aligned with the idea or experience on the EarthPlane of being in a meadow surrounded by wildflowers. There are trees in the distance and the sun is soaking into you. In the Light, our meadow is a bit different, but we first wanted to conjure up this vision, so you could see it in your mind's eye prior to further explaining how the soul rests when it is having this experience.

Firstly, it is important to note that the Meadow is located in the PlantRealm, which is a realm within the Multiverse (encompassing all the Universes). The PlantRealm intersects with the Light at a certain juncture—just as the edge of a forest meets with the meadow located next to it. A soul enters the PlantRealm from the LightPlane for deep soul healing and rejuvenation. This occurs at regular intervals during one's ascension while in the Light. This deep, soul level plant healing is of vital importance to the function of the soul. The result of spending time in the Plant-Realm is that a soul experiences a bump-up in vibrational output. One's energetic output becomes higher frequency after a visit to the Meadow.

In the Meadow, as in a laboratory on the EarthPlane, souls involve themselves in experiments. The experiments are active in nature—the soul is involved in an "energetic" sense. Imagine you are in a field of flowers and a giant butterfly comes up to you and begins sipping nectar from your crown chakra. The vision may make you smile and even giggle, but at the same time we urge you to imagine what the connection of the butterfly sipping from your crown chakra might look and feel like.

The picture is a lovely one. At the same time, it is symbolic of your plant-based-soul-self connecting with your Light-Plane-based-self. Herein lies the secret to what is occurring in such an interchange. It is, of course, a melding of sorts, but at the same time it is an opportunity to learn from the PlantRealm, as both parties "download" information.

For this interchange to work and help both parties involved, it must be reciprocal. The PlantRealm and its representatives, in this instance, primarily Mother and Father Earth (but it can involve many others), are obtaining their own important downloads from the Light. Think of this information as a news update.

The soul being healed by the PlantRealm is offering up information about what is occurring in the Light for that particular soul. This information is recorded in the PlantRealm databank.

Note: An interesting aside of significance regarding the Plant-Realm when a soul is in human form. Plant DNA is very similar to human DNA.

A soul does a bit of tinkering in the Meadow, as well. It is like your workshop or garage on the EarthPlane. Here the soul has free reign to try "new and different" experiences. It is a safe realm and highly guarded from infiltration from other realms and dimensions. This is where the soul can truly frolic in a field of daisies if the soul chooses. And being a place of rest, the soul finds the necessary nurturing that allows it to rest, which enables further expansion and exploration once the soul emerges from the Meadow.

THE HIGH COURT

While this doesn't sound like a place of rest by human standards, it is a place of rest in the LightPlane. If you are supposing or guessing this is a place where the "higher echelons" in the Light congregate, we once again say yes and no. Unlike the EarthPlane, where the higher echelons are ensconced in the High Court and no "underlings" are allowed to enter (unless on a subservient basis), in the Light, all souls spend their time in the High Court. When and how, we will explain.

First, we will give you an idea of the appearance of the High Court within the Light. The High Court looks similar to a medieval high court on the EarthPlane. There is a throne, of sorts, surrounded by an effervescent, smoky cloud of shimmering light. There is one chair for the soul that has been assigned to the throne, and a giant host of Angels surround the throne. While the soul does not actually sleep as you do on the EarthPlane, just being on the throne gives the soul a deep rest, for the soul is alternately healed and infused with further knowledge by the tremendous host of Angels surrounding the throne. So, in this sense, it is a very restful and powerful experience. One of the most powerful in the Universe!

When You Go to the High Court

You go to the High Court at intervals throughout your soul ascension. The determinants as to when that will occur could be likened to an algebraic equation. There is much that goes into this determination. Given the many souls that exist, this is not an occasion that occurs very often in one's soul journey. It happens at certain points on the ladder of ascension, which are pivotal in nature. When one is in preparation for a soul task, or when one is about to take on a master status of some sort, such as Ascended Master or life guide, those occasions would necessitate a visit to the High Court.

How Do You Get to the High Court?

The journey to the High Court is instantaneous. However, the preparation is not. It takes many months and often years by EarthPlane standards to prepare for your visit to the High Court. Yet when it is time, you arrive in the High Court chair in less than a split second.

How Long Does the High Court Experience Last?

By EarthPlane standards, it would be similar to a month. However, remember that time is very different in the Light. Therefore, if you were to see it happen, it would seem much faster. It is difficult for us to explain, as the difference in time between the EarthPlane and the Light is great. The reason for this is tied into the frequency at which energy vibrates in the Light. It is exponentially much higher and faster in the Light than on the EarthPlane.

Is there a set time that each soul spends in the Court? Although the time spent is similar for each soul, it does vary slightly. It is all calibrated to the soul's need and for whatever the soul is experiencing at that moment and place in time.

A SOUL'S PERSONAL PLACE OF REST

At this juncture, you no doubt have begun to wonder if one has a personal space—akin to the bedroom and bed on the EarthPlane. You may have thought that such a place doesn't exist, but it does. Here is where souls go to simply rest for however long by Light-Plane standards is necessary. On Earth, this could be mere moments, or it could span months. We know this is very confusing—this issue of time being so much different there than here—but it is as it is. Suffice it to say you get the adequate amount of rest your soul requires while in your personal place of rest.

Unlike the other locations, here you simply rest, re-energize and reinvigorate your various energetic systems. In that regard it is much like one's bedroom on Earth. It is of course different in its own right, but before we cover those differences, we will answer a question we hear lingering with you, and that is how often a soul spends in the personal place of rest compared to the other rejuvenation locations mentioned previously. If we are to give you a percentage, we would have to say that one rests 88.88 percent of the time in one's personal place of rest.

Where the remaining percentage is spent depends on your soul journey and soul path and any major agendas coming from the Light or Multiverse. For souls must sometimes enter projects as needed and required, and then this remaining percentage will change and is therefore always in a state of flux. For example, one could attend a challenging meeting with other souls in another galaxy, and then return and require time in the Incubator. Or one could venture out into the Multiverse and return with knowledge that needs to be understood and assimilated in the Library, and potentially stored there. We believe you get the picture, as they say.

What the Personal Place of Rest Looks and Feels Like

Not surprisingly, or surprisingly, the Personal Place of Rest is very personal. Meaning that what it looks and feels like is somewhat different for each soul—much like one's bedroom/place of rest is different. However, there are some similarities. The place of rest is comforting in its own right. By that we mean it allows for supreme relaxation, and in that regard it features a lot of what you call white on the EarthPlane. It has a white, cloudlike effect— for white and hazy white, which have the look and feel of a cloud, are something you will see in the Light.

This may seem a surprise in some regard, as it is often depicted as such, and you may be wondering, is it possible souls have seen this accurately while on the EarthPlane? We will give you a resounding yes. That is not to say that all the Light is white and ethereal looking as you have surmised and represented it, but the Personal Place of Rest is often like this. White is a supreme, all-knowing color, and while color is different in the Light, in some regards it is the same. The soul will align and subscribe to certain colors and color tones, and white as an all-knowing and all-being color is somewhat universal in this regard.

You may be simultaneously wondering how this place "feels" to the touch. You might think it is soft, as you often arrange your sleeping place to be this way. However, the sense of touch is entirely different in the Light compared to the EarthPlane. There is a sense of softness and lightness in such a place in the LightPlane, but there is not the same tactile feeling of softness, as with a very soft fur, for instance, or silk sheets. But one has a sense of softness. In this area of touch, it is very different yet the same here in the Light. By different, we mean the experience is entirely different, yet the overall feeling and the result is the same. One feels a place of rest as soft, if not by touch, then by feeling. We do hope you can wrap your EarthPlane mind around this.

What occurs during this personal place of resting? You may be wondering if you dream as you do on the EarthPlane. Firstly, we would like to explain a few things about dreaming, such as it is on the EarthPlane. When you dream on the EarthPlane, you are often visiting the LightPlane. Here in the LightPlane, souls come together to commune and communicate and make plans for initiatives and conquests, and even prepare for and set out for those conquests. If you wake up feeling like you have engaged in battle, you have! Your soul, that is. So, are dreams ever just dreams —wanderings of the mind? Yes, a percentage of dreams are just dreams. A chance for your mind to do its own wandering and "what ifs" trying things on for size. As for the percentage, if we are to give you one, we would say that 33.3 percent of your dreams are simply mind-wanderings, while the remaining are visits to the Light and even other Galaxies while you "sleep."

Returning to the question of whether you dream in the Light —you do not. Rather, you are constantly being energized by your sleep.

OTHER SPACES FOR SOULS

In the human realm, as you well know, you have your own personal spaces for more than just sleep and rest. You are well aware of these spaces, but we will enumerate them here and then cover whether there is something similar to these spaces in the Light.

1. **Bathroom/loo.** Let's cover this first. No, there is no need for physical actions such as using the toilet or bathing one's physical body here, so we really don't have any loos, as they say, here!
2. **Living room.** We shall include this with the family room. Yes, we do have locations where souls can

gather, but no, each soul does not have his or her own living room in which to do this—at least not in the way you are used to. Rather, when a soul wishes to gather other souls together, the soul simply sends out an energetic frequency and that frequency then informs all who are invited as to where and when. The "where" will be where it is appropriate based on the messaging to be shared. Hence, it is much like calling a board meeting and asking that all attendees report to a certain location at a certain time. You may be thinking, why don't souls just hang about and enjoy one another as is done on the EarthPlane? The answer is we do commune, but we do so with intent and purpose in mind. If you are thinking that our souls are rather busy, you would be correct!

3. **Dining room.** As you are likely suspecting, we don't "eat" here like you do on the EarthPlane. No physical body, therefore, no need to fuel the physical body as you do there. We would be feasting on knowledge, so to speak, and sharing that knowledge with one another.

4. **Kitchen.** Ditto from above. Not necessary here on the LightPlane!

5. **Dressing room.** We don't dress as you have likely surmised.

6. **Garage.** Where to park our space vehicles? Perhaps in the garage? This is a bit of a joke, as you might realize. We don't require vehicles to get around here, as we move on energetic pathways, highways and byways.

7. **Mudroom.** No need for one. We don't muddy or dirty our shoes, as we don't wear shoes.

8. **Den/study/library.** Indeed! We do have the equivalent of these places. They are for studying purposes and for communing with one another in terms of sharing information.

COLOR AS A WAY TO ENVISION WHAT IT "LOOKS" LIKE HERE IN THE LIGHT

What do these various places look like, you are likely wondering? Let us explain, once again, about color. For that is the best way we can describe to you what things look like here.

Envision that our landscape is comprised of various colors. Not necessarily all colors of your rainbow, but there are colors that are prominent in the Light. These colors include white, as already mentioned, and various shades of blue and green. There may also be shades and hues of pink and purple, as guided by the preferences of individual souls.

So how does this work? These colors and preferences? For one, in addition to the personal resting place, there are areas of communal living and being where we have predominantly white. Sometimes a clear, bright light and at other times a more ethereal smoky or misty white. In fact, white is the most predominant color here. However, we do have other colors, as mentioned, and they are often associated with other locations here in the Light.

Blue is used primarily in communication zones of the Light. For instance, in the Akashic and Great Libraries and other libraries of importance here. Blue is also used in the Resolution Zone where solutions are reached when souls veer off their course into the course of another soul.

Green is a healing color, and so it is prominent in healing areas, such as the Incubator. While there are varying shades of green on the EarthPlane, we will not drill down too much on types and shades of color, for it could become overwhelming. We will suffice it to say that the deeper you envisage a color when you are reading this and tapping into what the LightPlane "looks" like, the more powerful the location is and the more soul energies are often present in that location. It is as if a giant paintbrush might apply a swath of color onto some of these locations. The energetic vibration will be quite loud at times, and so the color will be deeper.

Here in the Light, the various hues do hold their own energetic vibrations and frequencies. In fact, each is much different than another. Hence the different ways of being in each space and the different ways of experiencing. On the EarthPlane, you use color to indicate one way of being—and that is when someone is "feeling blue." Here in the Light, color is much more all-encompassing and offers a quite magnificent way for you on Earth to envision and see the Light in your mind's eye.

As we continue to explore color here in the Light, we shall bring up what you call **orange**. You might think of it as quite a garish color, but here in the Light it is considered a vibrant color full of promise. A major reason for this is that orange is the color that springs forth when soul-seeds spark and germinate. Yes, another concept here of utmost significance that we will now cover!

WHEN SOUL-SEEDS SPARK

We all come from a soul-seed spark. There are different variations of the soul-seed spark, depending on in which dimension one springs forth, but suffice it to say that it all starts with the soul-seed spark, and the soul-seed spark is an orange conflagration of color when this process occurs! We know we are digressing here a bit, as this is not of the landscape, but it is something important to mention, and we will be going into a bit more detail about this in the third section of this book, as it does affect the convergence of the Light and the EarthPlane.

If you meditate after reading this and find you are able to see brief flashes of the Light, or even tour the Light as you "sleep" in human form, you will see various sections or bastions of orange light as you go on your journey, which indicate those locations where soul-seeds are germinating. Or if the light is a "mounded light" that appears to be pulsating or there are orange sparks, this may indicate that the sparking (birthing) process is occurring.

You may be thinking that it would seem logical to have germinating and birthing occur in a specific location or locations. It is a bit more sporadic and chaotic here—or it may seem to be so. In fact, it is all preplanned and extraordinarily "at one." By that we mean that if you were to map things out, you would see that the soul germination and sparking create an intricate pattern within the Light.

We remind you that it is all simply energy here. Therefore, energetic pathways look quite different to the EarthPlane's web of hospitals and birthing centers within those hospitals. And even when birthing occurs outside of the hospital, as it does throughout the world, the process is generally assigned to a certain location within the framework of the society in which the birthing is taking place. But it is different in the Light.

Now to answer a question that may be swirling around in your mind. What about the color black? For on the EarthPlane in some cultures, black is not considered to be a "good" color—and may be representative of death and even what you call "evil." **Black** is also a conglomeration of many colors, and in that regard, it is not really anything. So, black is not represented here in the Light, for we are always lit up—if that makes sense. We do not have the dark nights you have on the EarthPlane. There is no need or even the ability to "shut off the lights" here. For this is the "Light."

There are secondary colors here. Colors you may not consider secondary on the EarthPlane, yet nonetheless are secondary here. For as you will see when we explain color to you in terms of our vocabulary, it does not have the same consequence as it has for you on the EarthPlane. In keeping with our goal to give you a clear idea of our landscape here, we will cover a few more of our secondary or minor colors with a short description for each.

Pink is heart-centered here in the Light, as it often is on the EarthPlane. We have a very faint pink that some souls emit when they greet one another. A sort of embrace with color and the energetic pathways and blips of light that erupt when two likeminded souls "run into each other" in the Light as if by happenstance.

Not surprisingly, however, there is no "chance" here. We move with great intent and purpose and know when we are meeting up with other souls. However, our LightPlane selves are not so different that we aren't happy to see one another. The light pink rays we emit are proof of the pleasure in seeing and being akin to one another in a soul sense.

Mauve/purple: We say mauve, for the color here looks more like your mauve than your deeper purple. It serves as our purple here. Often on the EarthPlane purple is considered a spiritual color. Here in the Light you will find areas that are a light mauve —this tends to be in the communal living areas where knowledge is shared.

Gray: We don't have much gray here. Perhaps gray appears for moments in time as colors that show up meld, but then it is gone.

Of course, there are many other colors you have in your rainbow that may or may not show up here. Rather than belaboring the point, we will sign off from this aspect, as we feel that you have a picture in terms of color present here. And, so, we shall move on.

IS THERE SOUND IN THE LIGHT?

Sound is much different in the Light than the EarthPlane. Whereas the EarthPlane has distinct sounds that transmit certain feelings and messages, in the Light it is more about the vibration of sound, which is essentially the transmission of energy.

Souls in the Light communicate through thought patterns best described as the high-pitched, high-frequency click sounds made by whales and dolphins on the EarthPlane. While these high-pitched sound waves would not be recognizable to the human ear, they are readily understood from soul to soul within the Light. If you were to stand and listen in the Light while in human form, the best way we can describe the experience is that you would hear a faint buzzing and sizzling sound, as you might hear on a quiet night from nearby electrical poles.

WHAT IS TIME ON THE OTHER SIDE AND HOW IT RELATES TO EARTHPLANE OBJECTIVES

Of all concepts, time is most certainly one of the most confusing and confounding for humans. For time does not exist in the Light as it exists on the EarthPlane. Some say there is no time here, but that is not true. There is time here. It is just very different from time on the EarthPlane. Some have said that time is not linear or chronological here as it is on the EarthPlane. That would be true, but there is even more to the aspect of time in the Light. For on the EarthPlane, time is closely tied into one's objectives, including life purpose and life path. The same holds true in the Light, where time is also interconnected with the various paths of souls. We shall attempt to explain this in a way that you will understand in the following passage.

Let us start with a definition of time on the EarthPlane and then juxtapose this with a definition here in the Light. This will help you digest this rather "large" aspect of time.

TIME ON THE EARTHPLANE

Time on the EarthPlane is a linear, chronological aspect of being alive. It is something that moves one from Point A to Point B or even Point Z. Time holds various aspects of the EarthPlane together, as if a hinge or building block. Time keeps things in order on the EarthPlane and helps those living the human existence keep themselves in order, as well.

TIME IN THE LIGHT

Time in the Light, as mentioned, is very different than on the EarthPlane, and yet, it helps to keep souls in order. The order that time creates for souls in the Light has to do with soul path and soul purpose. For time is not linear or chronological in the Light, and indeed, time is not even measured here.

We can see you scratching your head, but bear with us. Here is a chronology of how time—in the sense you understand it on the EarthPlane—could work in the Light. It is much like a schedule, if that helps you understand.

1. An objective is identified by a soul.
2. The soul reviews the objective and its veracity— regarding how it resonates with the soul.
3. Auxiliary souls are identified and come forward and are asked if they are willing to participate in assisting the soul to achieve the objective.
4. The auxiliary souls to be involved in the objective are assigned their tasks and given a point in the process (time) when they will step in and do what they have agreed to do.
5. The objective is initiated.
6. The soul begins the predetermined/prescribed journey. (All of this is in unison and simultaneously accomplished together with a soul's other objectives. In the case of very all-encompassing, "grand" objectives, there will be less going on at once.)
7. At the set points predetermined, the soul stops on occasion, or changes course. This includes meeting up with souls who have come to assist.
8. At the point that the objective is met, which is a certain point that can be described as time, the met objective is recorded in the soul's record of self, also sometimes referred to as the Akashic Record.

THE APPARENT CHALLENGES OF THE LIGHTPLANE EXISTENCE

We will at this juncture touch on a point that may be occurring to you. And that is how erratic and haphazard the LightPlane may appear to souls on the EarthPlane, where time governs all things, and schedules and structure must prevail. While it may seem as if we are rushing around here and there without a plan here in the Light, we are not. It is just appearing so to you, as we don't have time and timelines that are chronological, as mentioned previously. And this does tend to make things look as if it is a bit of a "mess." But it is not, we assure you.

As mentioned in the LightPlane timeline above, each soul directs the soul journey. Therefore, there is a plan, and it is not haphazard. It is an individual plan for every individual soul. We do hope that this is clear. You may be reminded at this juncture of someone in your life who appears quite haphazard and disorganized yet seems to get done what needs to be done, anyway. If that helps you accept and understand, then we do suggest you use this analogy.

ARE THERE SCHEDULES ON THE OTHER SIDE? OR IS IT ALL FLUID?

We know that as humans you crave order, and from that comes the need for schedules and timing attached to those schedules. While schedules do keep you on course while on the EarthPlane, they don't necessarily do the same here. Although, as mentioned, there are schedules to achieve soul purpose objectives. We will do our best to describe schedules here. You will see they are a bit different, yet there are some similarities, the latter of which will help you in your pursuit of understanding how things work here in the Light.

Schedules are a construct created on the EarthPlane, and yet, there is a bit of scheduling that does occur here in the Light. This is how it works.

1. A higher being (your soul) decides on a pursuit of some sort—be that a new knowledge base or a deeper understanding of a concept. When this occurs, all who can help in this endeavor are—in the best way we know of describing this—telepathically alerted to your intention.
2. Once the alert goes out, those most required for the pursuit are summoned to a "meeting of the minds." This is a virtual meeting of a sort that occurs rather instantaneously.
3. During this meeting, which may be rather brief by EarthPlane standards, everyone is assigned their specific task or tasks and can ask any clarifying questions as to their role in the pursuit. There is never —we feel this is important to mention—questions from one soul to the other about the purpose or relevance of the specific task, for all in the Light understand that a soul has his or her reasons, and there is no need to question those reasons, nor would it be welcome, nor sanctioned in any way whatsoever here in the Light.
4. While there is no overriding judgment of the process, there is someone guiding the process, and that someone is the soul. And when the soul permits and requests, the soul's life guide on the EarthPlane does weigh in. However, and this is a big however, this would only occur if the goal or part of the goal will be met by the soul while living out an existence on the EarthPlane. If this is not the case—if the soul expansion is primarily to be obtained within the Light or in another dimension—then the life guide would not step in.

5. Once the meeting of the various souls involved in the pursuit is complete, the soul and the life guide, if involved, "sit down" and review what has been proposed by the soul and how those souls called in will be fulfilling their ends of the bargain, so to speak. All is carefully recorded in a subsection of one's Akashic Record.

6. After the recording of information is complete, the soul visits his or her soul chair for programming and planning of the goal and lessons involved in the goal, and all that will be involved with the process. This is a chair that resembles on the EarthPlane a white ethereal throne on which the soul "downloads" the entire plan for the pursuit.

7. Once programming is complete, the soul sets out on the journey. You may be wondering at this point if that particular journey is the only one on which the soul does set out. The answer is no. A soul—and this is where it gets tricky for the human brain to understand—is undertaking various soul missions simultaneously. Is this a tumultuous, frenetic sort of journey, given all the moving pieces? No, it is not. At least in the human sense. For the soul can keep all of the proverbial balls in the air, and no information is lost or not attended to at any point in time. This is known as universal knowingness.

8. Once the journey is complete, the soul and life guide, if applicable, review what was learned and the knowledge and components gathered. While on the EarthPlane, such a review might include what went wrong along the way, but this does not occur in the Light. Rather, the soul will determine if what was learned was enough to obtain the particular lesson. If not, a new plan is determined and the cycle continues. If all is determined to be completed, at

that point, the soul may be able to see a bump up in status.

IS THERE PAIN ON THE OTHER SIDE?

As is known and understood on the EarthPlane, there is no physical pain here in the Light. Many who have died and returned to Earth will attest to the physical pain being nonexistent in their near-death experience. However, there is emotional pain on the EarthPlane, and in some instances that can be more debilitating for humans than physical pain. In this regard, you may be wondering if there is emotional pain in the Light. There are emotions in the Light. However, they are different and serve different purposes in the Light.

First, let's discuss emotions felt when a person on the Earth-Plane dies temporarily. You will hear those who have had near-death experiences say they felt emotions during their transition from Earth to the Light and then upon return to Earth. They will often say they experienced an extreme sense of peace and tranquility when they arrived in the Light and a resulting unwillingness to leave the Light when called back to the EarthPlane. These are all felt emotions. So, as you can see, these emotions do occur when in the Light. However, and this is an important distinction, those who experience a near-death experience are not completely "in" and "of" the Light during this experience. Instead, they are in a sort of netherworld where they are neither here nor there. That being said, the emotions they feel are not the same type or intensity of emotions felt when a person is completely in and of the Light. Those experiencing a near-death are still in human form, and so they sense and feel human emotions while in the Light.

Now that we have that explained, we will delve into what emotions look and feel like when you are completely in the Light. This is not an easy translation for you on the EarthPlane, as you are used to feelings being very visceral and affecting various areas of the physical body. Since we don't have a physical body here, that does not occur. However, feelings are felt—just in a different manner. Here we provide a look at the process, which we hope will help you understand it.

1. An occurrence tied into a soul's purpose occurs, which brings up a signal.
2. The signal relays a message to certain receptors within the soul's DNA circuitry.
3. When the signal is relayed, the soul immediately accesses all that was planned for the particular goal and all that was accomplished, and there is a quick check to ensure nothing remains lingering in terms of tasks to still complete.
4. Once this has all been accomplished, the soul feels a sense of something very similar to your satisfaction about a job well done on the EarthPlane. It is a deep and fulfilling sensation for the soul. The feeling also sends out a signal to those souls involved in the process that the job/pursuit/goal is complete to the satisfaction of the soul.
5. You may now be wondering if the soul then communicates with the souls involved to thank them, and the answer is a resounding yes. In fact, the souls generally commune to celebrate once the signal is sent out. While you may on the EarthPlane have a celebration of the physical, such as enjoying food and drink, in the Light, the celebration focuses on the accomplishment itself, the roles of all involved, and how the accomplishment also moved those involved along their soul paths.

You may be thinking this sounds like all work and no play. It does look that way by EarthPlane standards, but remember it is a different world here without the physical and the visceral feelings experienced because of the physical. Therefore, souls do not miss the physical aspect, because it doesn't exist. Rather, souls are focused on improving and attaining enlightenment (ascending), and in communing with one another in pursuit of ascension and a greater understanding of the inclusiveness yet separateness of the Multiverse. Our next section covers what communing entails.

COMMUNING IN THE LIGHT

You humans do use the word communing in a more "Light"-oriented sense, and so we are using this word to describe what goes on in the Light. A similar word is fellowship.

So, what does communing in the Light look like? Are there enjoyable aspects of this experience? Most certainly! In fact, souls in the Light look forward to this communing, and we do have a secret to share with you about this. Also in attendance at these events are Earthbound souls.

You may now be a bit perplexed at the previous statement. Let us clear things up for you. What is commonly referred to as your higher self is that part of you always in and of the Light. Therefore, all human souls are in essence always in the Light. That being said, since you are always in the Light, your soul attends many such communal functions in the Light. We will explain more about this process overall in the third section when we describe how the EarthPlane and the Light converge. Suffice it to say for now that your higher self attends these events, and your higher self revels in these experiences and gets much out of them.

Back to communing in the Light for those souls fully housed within the Light. What do they get out of communing?

Communing is an ethereal sort of experience, which likely doesn't surprise you. It is something that must, of course, be experienced to fully understand. But, as mentioned, we are doing our best to impart what it is like to you. Here is the general communing process.

1. It begins with a call—a sort of invitation to the party. At this call, the soul has a zing of what we shall refer to as satisfaction combined with anticipation at the call and the knowing that the "get together" will be an enjoyable and productive one.

2. Soon after, all souls report to the destination, which is generally a location within the Light where souls gather. You can think of this as a sort of meeting room held and rented out. Although no rent is due. But if this gives you a way to visualize.

3. The rooms from your perspective look as if they are filled with mist and generally consist of a white table, and chairs, although the chairs may or may not be present. For we souls in the Light generally don't need to sit. However, we may do so at times.

4. There are no snacks like you would have on the EarthPlane, for as mentioned, we do not experience the physical, per se. However, we may symbolically toast to grand ideas with something that appears like liquid refreshment and yet is of energetic frequency. This concoction is a mix of energetic frequencies of the souls who are toasting. If there are many souls, there will be many energetic frequencies attached to this toast. The toast is an acknowledgment of what has been accomplished, and the energies that combined to make the accomplishment a reality.

5. As for the length of these celebrations, once again it is difficult to compare to EarthPlane standards. Whereas you may have such a celebration that could last 3-4 hours, our celebrations from your perspective would be quite brief. But they are of sufficient length for what we are accomplishing, which is to celebrate a job well done and to acknowledge who was involved in the job well done. This is simply all that souls in the Light are interested in.

COMMUNING WITH SPECIFIC SOULS

There are tête-à-têtes, so to speak, that occur between individual souls in the Light. We know much has been shared on the Earth-Plane indicating we are all one in the Light. However, as mentioned previously in this book, that is somewhat of a misnomer. For, free will is the law of the Universe. Period. And therefore, free will does transcend the idea of being all and one. That being said, it is the case that souls do commune together one-on-one, overriding the notion of all being one. What is said and communicated during these conversations varies greatly between the souls who commune. We can't give you a complete list of what might occur, but we can share with you a list of items that do occur, to give you an idea.

1. Souls get together to discuss other souls. This is not in a "gossipy" way as occurs on the EarthPlane, but in a way that addresses how the souls speaking might assist the soul whom they are speaking of. Plans are made to assist that soul with ascension. When this occurs— this meeting of the minds—the soul being spoken about gets a sort of memo—think of it as an email or text message—that he or she is being spoken about and by whom and for what purpose.

2. Here is an interesting tidbit for you. Not that all of this isn't interesting! But this revelation is likely to surprise you. When souls commune in the Light, they often harken back to previous times together. While the LightPlane is one of forward movement, for the most part, souls look to what you would consider the past on the EarthPlane. Why do they do this? Not for sentimentality or to become nostalgic, per se. Rather, they look to the past to see how far they have come and what worked and what didn't as they have pursued their various goals and agendas during

ascension. In this regard, they use their past experiences as a "playbook."

3. Are there very special souls with whom you commune while in the Light? Like a partner on the EarthPlane or family member? Yes, there most certainly are. While these relationships are different than they are on the EarthPlane, in some ways they are the same. We will break things down here for you in terms of the similarities and differences.

SPECIAL SOUL BOND SIMILARITIES IN THE LIGHT AND ON THE EARTHPLANE

Souls possessing a special bond with one another while in the Light will likely have played out those special bonds on Earth. For instance, they may have married over many lifetimes or played the part of parent and child or sibling and sibling, etc. But which comes first? The deep connection or the partnering that leads to deep connection?

As it turns out, the connection is born during the soul spark. Why certain individuals are paired during this soul sparking is a complex matter linked to frequency bandwidth. There are soul spark frequencies that allocate souls to specific soul families. Soul families exist because it would simply not work on the EarthPlane or LightPlane to not organize souls in this manner. Chaos would reign supreme if all souls were connected in this very intimate way. Soul spark families allow for these deep connections in and out of the Light. These connections are why you gravitate toward certain souls more than others. It is also the reason things remain in order in the Light.

SPECIAL SOUL BOND DIFFERENCES IN THE LIGHT AND ON THE EARTHPLANE

The main difference between special soul bonds in the Light versus the EarthPlane is that these relationships are of and for the Light. By that we mean that while certain souls may love to commune with one another and seek comfort in the union in the Light, their sole purpose there is to help one another ascend.

Those souls with whom we bond in the Light are those souls aligned with our soul journey. It is not necessarily that our soul journey is equal or similar. In fact, in some cases the journeys are starkly different. This has more to do with the soul spark origin of the person and the particular energetic frequency that the person emits. To put this in human terms, think of energetic connectors as radio frequencies, such as in a walkie talkie system. You must be on the same frequency to communicate. Another analogy is the topic of pheromones. These are receptors sent out to call in others. This phenomenon occurs with many species on Earth, including humans and insects. Those who are on the same frequency in the Light send out a sort of pheromone to those within their same frequency.

This final portion of Part Two does provide a nice segue to Part Three, where we cover how the Light and the EarthPlane converge.

How the EarthPlane and the Other Side Converge

PART THREE

Now we come to the point in the book you have no doubt been looking forward to, as we will cover how our worlds coexist and at times collide. We will do our best to explain this in terms that make sense and resonate with you.

We will start with an explanation of how the EarthPlane is but one plane/location/existence that a soul in the Light can choose to experience. Yet it is considered one of the most difficult of "assignments," for there is a big jump downward vibrationally to become human—and to learn the lessons necessary to survive the Earth-Plane existence.

To become human is a notable task that requires much from the soul. Of course, the first question to ask of those on the Earth-Plane (many of whom have suffered in various degrees), is, "Why would you even want to bother with the EarthPlane experience, given its proclivity to be especially difficult?"

We will give you an example here drawn from the idea of going to school and higher learning. When you continue to climb in terms of education, you take on more complicated tasks within those learning experiences. If you were to complete an undergraduate program in the United States, for instance, you would then be ready to take courses that could lead to receiving a master's or PhD.

NEAR-DEATH EXPERIENCES

Certainly, near-death experiences, as they are called on the Earth-Plane, are a convergence of the Earth and the Light. In fact, they are a sort of collision. For when you are on the Earth and visit the LightPlane, even for a short time, you have collided with death, so to speak, or it could be argued—vice versa. At any rate, this rather profound human experience is a disruption to what is generally a seamless co-existence between the two planes. You have heard the term "Beyond the Veil," meaning the state of being beyond death. Moving from the EarthPlane to the LightPlane when you actually "die physically" is like passing through a simple veil.

But when you have a near-death experience, you don't have this seamless movement between Earth and the Veil. What occurs is a temporary state of being in the Light while still in the Earth-Plane body, though not completely. The body has often temporarily died or expired on the Earth so that the spirit could come to the Light like other spirits who have actually died on Earth. But it is a time-sensitive matter, to use an EarthPlane term. The near-death experience is just that—near death. Not complete. Instead, hanging over the edge of a precipice with your feet still planted on the ground.

We can see you understand this way of being "half in one realm" and "half in the other." But the question is, "Why does this occur, and how does it affect the EarthPlane physical body and more importantly, the soul?

We will now answer these questions and provide other salient, relevant, cogent, and vital information.

The near-death experience breeds faith in those on the Earth-Plane that there is more to the Earthbound life. On the one hand, this seems unnecessary. For although an individual might not "believe in" the afterlife or the Other Side while in the current incarnation of himself or herself on the Earth, when that soul returns to the Light, it becomes obvious they were incorrect about there being no afterlife. So, what is the point? As has been shared throughout this book, souls come to the Earth to learn certain soul lessons that cannot be learned anywhere else. Therefore, having a near-death experience expands your soul in a way that no other experience can. In the Light, there is no death, and therefore a soul would be unable to have such an experience. However, while on Earth, one can "die" and experience a rebirth of sorts, which expands the soul.

We hear you wondering, "Why bother going to the Earth to experience all the trials and tribulations the EarthPlane brings? Wouldn't it be easier to just forgo those trials and tribulations, including the sorrow, pain and loss that accompany the Earth-Plane existence?" The LightPlane sounds so freeing and enjoyable to those who are currently Earthbound. "Why not just stay in the Light and expand there in a more pleasant environment?" For there are opportunities to expand within the Light, correct? Yes and no. As mentioned, there are simply no other "opportunities" for expansion within the Universe such as those that exist on the EarthPlane. Here is more explanation of this topic.

HOW NEAR-DEATH EXPERIENCES AFFECT THE EARTHPLANE BODY

First, which is of concern to medical professionals, the near-death experience, and specifically the lack of oxygen to the brain and blood system and cells, may have life-altering effects on the physical body. Whether this will occur is not so much a function of the near-death experience itself, but a function of what the soul is attempting to achieve or learn from the near-death experience.

That being said, if a soul was planning to experience a physical disability where none existed before in this particular lifetime, then effects from the lack of oxygen, heart pumping incorrectly, etc., would come into play. If, on the other hand, the soul wishes to experience the lesson that "death" does not truly exist and that souls come to the EarthPlane to simply house themselves within physical bodies that are in fact somewhat like empty shells when the soul is not actively occupying them—then the physical body would simply jump back into life, so to speak, and no lingering effects from being "dead" would be evident.

HOW IS THE SOUL AFFECTED BY THE HARDSHIPS OF THE EARTHPLANE?

The next question for you may very likely be, "If the EarthPlane existence is such a stressful and painful one—notwithstanding the joys and triumphs that come with it, but looking at the "hard" parts of living an EarthPlane existence—how does that affect the soul in the long run, given the fact that souls continue to return to the EarthPlane after a near-death experience?"

While we would like to say there is no "damage" to the soul during these sojourns, the truth is that it can be hard on your soul to continue to reincarnate. This begs the question then—is it even safe to do so? The fact is that it is safe to do so, but often souls need a rest in between lifetimes. Often that rest can be many years by EarthPlane standards. The soul may also spend some time in the LightPlane Incubator in recovery. We hear you asking once again, "Why bother with the EarthPlane if recovery is needed?" We will cover next in more detail the reasons the EarthPlane is an important aspect of expanding one's soul, which is something we have already covered to some extent.

While the LightPlane does afford one the opportunity to expand, it is not a—for lack of a better way to say this—"nitty-gritty" experience in the Light. For one thing, there is no physical pain, nor emotional torment. While both these factors are often dreaded for good reason when one is an Earthbound soul, they are great teachers. There are a multitude of lessons that these teachers can teach. Here are just a few for your perusal.

Opportunity to Feel Emotions

In the EarthPlane existence, emotions are quite a "large" aspect of living for humans. And those emotions affect many aspects of living—both emotional and physical. For when one has an extreme emotional reaction it affects the physical—and vice versa. This push and pull with emotions can lead to great soul expansion.

Compassion for Other Souls

In many other locations within the Multiverse, there is not the breadth of knowledge and emotions as there is on the Earth. For those who have suffered from similar circumstances and plights, and for souls in general, suffering may lead to understanding and compassion. For in human form, souls do suffer similar circumstances.

Ability to Navigate the Many Planes and Dimensions of the Multiverse

The EarthPlane existence, which is accepted in the Light as one of the most difficult "assignments" in the Universe, makes one more capable of not only navigating the EarthPlane, but also navigating other planes and dimensions within the Multiverse.

The Experience of Physical Pain and Physical Pleasure

While both pain and pleasure can be extreme at times, they provide opportunities to simply feel the physical. You may ask, "Why is this of importance if physical pain is not experienced in the Light? Why bother with physical pain when it is not a part of existence within our true home in the Light?"

Physical pain, while it does not exist in the Light, broadens your soul. Therefore, it is of consequence in and out of the Light.

For when you endure physical pain on the EarthPlane, you generally have a "soul expansion" experience of some sort—even if that soul-expanding experience is to discover that the true self is not of the physical body, but of the soul.

As for pleasure, the same is true. The soul on the EarthPlane expands in its ability to enjoy physical pleasure. This may seem like the antithesis of growth, especially in light of the human expression of, "No pain, no gain," but pleasurable physical sensations also expand one's consciousness. For it is pleasurable physical sensations that cause a soul to access what is deep and abiding, in terms of connecting with its soul and soul purpose.

When you feel pleasure on the EarthPlane, you access serotonin and other pleasure receptors in the body, and may experience joy, love, ecstasy, and other positive emotions, including states of spiritual awareness such as are involved in meditation, for example. So, for these facets of human experience, a soul might choose to come to the EarthPlane. Pleasure may also, of course, be found in sexual activities, which are not available on the Other Side or in many other places in the Multiverse.

Despite a common misconception in some communities on the EarthPlane that pleasure is not desirable and should therefore not be encouraged, the human experience is designed to offer both pain and pleasure, and therefore pleasure should not, and indeed is not, discounted by your soul—for both teach lessons.

We will mention sexual pleasure here, for this is a sore spot for many, as according to various belief systems on the EarthPlane, it is considered not "of the Light." This is something that some of you may have a hard time understanding. We ask that you try to untangle what you were taught in terms of organized religion and approach this from a more analytical perspective. If you are able to do this, you will see that it "makes sense."

A soul that decides to enter human form is doing so for several reasons, with two main reasons being to experience the human experience that includes both pleasure and pain, including emotional pain. It takes another leap of understanding here to realize that it is not because the soul seeks the experience itself. It is because the soul seeks the knowledge and understanding that comes from experiencing the physical, and this can include being an observer or a participant in carnage, where humans bestow harm upon one another.

As we have already mentioned on several occasions, the Earth-Plane is the only place in the Multiverse that offers the physical experience in this profound way. We know this will involve another leap of faith, but, yes, souls do seek the knowledge that comes from carnage, including wars, famine, and one human harming another human.

Once again, we ask that you set aside human judgment here—for this will not be understood if you do not. We ask that you think of human existence as a video game, if you will. One plays video games where there can be much carnage as the two (or more) sides duel or engage in combat. When you are in the Light and setting up your lifetimes that will take place in the physical world, you may also decide if you would like to take part in the various planned physical experiences of carnage on the EarthPlane.

Once again, you do this to have the experience so that your soul can expand. Such soul expansion may include increasing compassion, or it could be something less obviously connected, such as increasing intimacy between souls. Souls that survive carnage together will become more intimate. In this case, intimacy refers not to sexual relations—although sex may very well come from the intimacy experienced on Earth—but is more concerned with the overall idea of intimacy that creates bonds between souls nothing can break.

SOULMATES

The idea of soulmates is a popular topic amongst those in human form. Indeed, it has "significance" in the Light as well.

Soulmates are just as the name suggests. Mates for the soul.

That being said, they are in essence closer to each other than other souls may be. This occurs because such souls tend to resonate with one another. Whereas the resonance on the EarthPlane may include physical or sensual enjoyment such as holding hands and walking along the beach, the satisfaction of souls mating in the Light has to do with "understanding" and the sharing of that understanding—which brings forth a resonance in each other's soul.

Suffice it to say that soulmates are indeed souls who resonate with each other and unite, and the union of their souls has a powerful influence throughout the Multiverse. For this reason, when two souls unite on the EarthPlane and are then separated by the physical "death" of the other, or there is a geographical distance between the two over some time, there can be an overwhelming sense of loss felt by the soul left behind, and in some respects also by the soul who is physically distant.

What of souls who have left, and furthermore, souls who have been separated? What is the significance of this very real occurrence that those on the EarthPlane experience? Why, for instance, does this occur? And how does this occurrence help one's soul journey? For wouldn't it be "better" by EarthPlane standards for the souls to simply co-exist with one another during the entirety of their EarthPlane existence and indeed existences? That way they could learn from one another and encourage one another.

Once again, the answer to this question is yes and no. Yes, the two souls could most definitely coexist on the EarthPlane for the near entirety of their journeys, and yes, because they are "kindred" souls, so to speak, they could learn lessons together that would expand their soul journeys, and indeed this does occur. On the other hand, there are lessons that can only be learned from the experience of being pulled apart physically from one another. As an earthly being, we know you have experienced this in one form or another. Be it a separation from a soulmate of the romantic sort or a soulmate of a platonic nature —such as a sibling, child, parent, or dear friend. And you may not have liked the experience, but you know deep in your soul that there were lessons that came from the separation. Lessons that "smarted" and lessons that made you grieve—but lessons, nonetheless.

What then are some of the lessons that separation from soulmates brings forth? We will enumerate them here for you.

1. Knowledge that although there is physical separation —spiritual, energetic separation never occurs.
2. The opportunity to experience pain at a soul level brought on by physical separation on the EarthPlane. When one has experienced on the EarthPlane that "come togetherness" in the physical sense, it can be wrenching in a physical, spiritual and emotional sense to have that torn from one's side. Why is this of significance? Because this type of soul wrenching expands the soul. We know this seems surprising, but it is in fact something that occurs. This is not to say that wonderful experiences by EarthPlane standards can't also mold the soul, but those soul-wrenching experiences have their own way of molding the soul.
3. A soul wishes to traverse the EarthPlane alone to understand at a soul level what it means to tap into one's soul journey on an individual level—free of "interference" from another. At times, it is necessary to take a solo journey to the center of the soul experience and to understand certain lessons on an individual soul level. Sometimes the soul will choose this experience throughout one's life—that of being without soulmates—but often it is something experienced for periods of time—though extended— rather than entire lifetimes. This occurs because it is difficult in human form to rise above an extended period of aloneness. There are junctures where a coming together of two like-hearted and like-minded

souls is necessary to effectively continue the soul journey.

LIFE GUIDES

A most divine convergence of the Light and the EarthPlane exists through one's life guide. Such souls sign up to go to the Earth-Plane with other souls to guide them. These souls know the entire life script of the soul to whom they have assigned themselves, and as such are able to effectively help guide the soul. In fact, they have had a hand in helping to write that life script. This relationship between the life guide and soul is a most intricate process that we will expound upon so you can gain a greater understanding of the vital role of your life guide.

First, we will discuss the life guide relationship and then how the life guide helps to steer you toward your higher purpose and soul mission.

Regarding the life guide and the purpose of the life guide, we'll begin with how two souls connect for this very special relationship. Firstly, we must share that every human has a life guide. You may not know or even have felt or sensed your life guide—at least not in the traditional sense—but we assure you that you have one.

Do some souls go through lifetimes without ever consciously accessing their life guides? Yes, they do. You may now be wondering and asking yourself, well, then, what is the purpose of the life guide? The purpose is that the life guide will guide—even when the human does not sense, see or know about the life guide. Because the life guide relationship with the soul is a relationship borne of the Light and essentially stays within the Light —not only throughout a soul's journey on the EarthPlane. There is also a connection (in the Light) when the human returns to the Light. However, we need to make it clear that the life guide only "functions" as a guide when the soul reincarnates into human form. When both are within the Light, consulting will occur at various junctures, but the life guide is not called upon for the constant support that is required on the EarthPlane.

You may be wondering what the life guide does if the soul decides to stay in the Light for an extended period of time. Not surprisingly, the life guide doesn't just sit around and wait. Rather, the life guide uses the "free" time for what you would call on the EarthPlane continuing education. As an ascended soul and Light Worker, the life guide needs to keep up with the "latest" happenings in the spiritual realm, just as they would on the EarthPlane.

As has been mentioned, the life guide is a supremely important connection to which two souls agree. How this agreement takes place is different for each soul duo, and yet there are similarities. We will begin with the similarities, for there are several.

The two souls who connect in the life guide-student union are two souls who have reincarnated together on the EarthPlane at some point. The timing as to how long it takes a soul to become another's life guide varies, but the fact that the two souls have reincarnated together is something that always occurs. They must both have lived on Earth as humans together at some point and developed a deep connection.

Often, the last lifetime in which the two souls were in human form is a pivotal and profound one. As such, it is helpful if you can tap into that lifetime, as it will reveal the nature of your connection with your life guide. Generally, in this final lifetime together on the EarthPlane, the connection is one of student and guide. This occurs because the person who becomes a life guide is more advanced ascension-wise than the soul who is guided.

This brings up a particular question to address at this juncture. If the purpose of the soul is to ascend, then what happens if the soul that has been guided by a life guide decides to become a life guide? In that case—and this would be the only case—the life guide-student contract is completed. At that point, the soul who has been a life guide will either: a) Find another soul to guide, or

b) No longer be a life guide, but rather look toward a "higher calling," such as an Ascended Master or Archangel.

A life guide and the soul with whom the life guide pledges allegiance tend to be aligned in many ways. This refers to their standing on the EarthPlane, as well as their standing in the Light. This is akin to those souls with whom we align as soulmates, yet, not surprisingly, it is a much deeper connection.

How is this connection different? While it is difficult to explain this deeper connection, it is not impossible, and so we'll attempt to do so. This deeper connection starts at a soul spark level. The individual with whom you align to guide you is someone with whom you have sparked into existence during the same set of soul sparks. Though this is a rather complicated process, suffice it to say that you were created in a specific "batch." That being said, you have similar soul DNA threads, strands, and occurrences. This is not to say that you will and have spent each and every moment in human form at the same time together, but it is to say that you came from the same origin.

When on the EarthPlane together, you will have been aligned in many fundamental ways. These include at a soul level in terms of those higher purpose goals to which you both ascribe. This also includes values and ways of being and even forms of communication.

HOW TO ACCESS YOUR LIFE GUIDE

Now we will discuss how you may access your life guide in this incarnation of yourself on the EarthPlane. Doing so helps expand your soul journey and experience on the EarthPlane as a human.

It may very well be that you have already accessed your life guide. If you have—congratulations. What we have to say here may help you expand that knowledge and get even more out of the divine connection. If you haven't yet accessed your life guide, this information will help you connect and experience the profound wisdom and knowledge that doing so can give you.

First, we will discuss the benefits of accessing one's life guide.

- You learn about the plans you made for yourself while still in the Light before you came to the EarthPlane. Though your life guide won't tell you about plans in the future you choose not to know yet, he or she will tap you into plans that your higher self would very much like you to know at this time. Often this occurs when you are at a crossroads of expansion and ascension in life. At this point, you will be trying to decide on next steps, and you may wish for guidance from your life guide.
- You learn you are truly never alone. Yes, it is known you have a cadre of souls to whom you can call on and rely on—such as loved ones who have passed on, people on the EarthPlane with you now, and Archangels and Ascended Masters—the list goes on. At the same time, these souls are connected, but they are not as connected as your life guide. A life guide truly is like a second skin in terms of being so closely tied to you that in this instance it is a case of where you begin and your life guide begins and ends. This is not to say that your life guide isn't his or her own person, but it is to say that the role they have taken on as your life guide is a sacred one that requires they literally climb into your soul in order to guide you. Think of your life guide as an inner compass—a built-in GPS to get you where you wish to go. Your life guide is not a separate entity in this lifetime, but rather a part of your entity. This is why your life guide may not be easy to detect—for he or she is so much a part of your soul at this point. This is not the case in the Light—but it is so during the human existence.
- You come to understand there is much support from the Light and the Multiverse for reaching toward your

soul purposes. While your life guide is the locus of control in terms of steering you in the right direction, such a sacred, completely protected union shows you that there is infinite support for you.

- Your life guide is in essence your lifeguard. He or she knows when you will be in danger—at what touchpoints in your life. As such, he or she will warn you when you are in danger and steer you to safety. You have likely been in circumstances in your life when you could have been harmed, but you were somehow steered clear of harm. That was your life guide guiding you to safety. This can be physical safety and it can be emotional safety, and even spiritual safety. So, you will know when you are guided, especially when it feels very internal, as if the advice is coming from deep within yourself. That is your life guide coming to the rescue!

HOW TO ACCESS YOUR LIFE GUIDE MOST EFFECTIVELY

Before we discuss how you can most effectively access your life guide, we must point out that "believing you have a life guide" is required to do this. Because life guides act as a second skin and are a part of you, it is often hard, as mentioned, for those in human form to ascertain and sense that a life guide is present. For this reason, many will say they don't believe they have a life guide. For certainly, if they did, wouldn't the life guide jump out or up and present himself or herself in a way that could and would be noticed?

The answer to this question is not surprisingly—yes and no. Yes, a life guide will present himself or herself, and sometimes in a way that is quite bold. But unless the individual is open to receiving messages from the Light—that individual is likely to miss the signs. You may have seen this occur when you are with "less enlightened souls." (Here we are referring to those souls in human form who have yet to tap in, or to tap in extensively, to the Light.) You may be watching such a soul go about his or her day and you notice the magical occurrences swirling around them. For instance, the butterfly following them down the street, the bluejay that stops and stares at them as they sit with their morning coffee, and the signs and synchronicities that present themselves to them via other people and circumstances. And yet, the person, if not tapped in, will not notice these occurrences, or if they notice them, they will not see them as signs and synchronicities, but just occurrences or coincidences—albeit often happy ones.

If you are wondering if you have a life guide, do take heed of what was just mentioned in the previous paragraph, and begin to pay attention to your surroundings and what is occurring in your surroundings and who or what presents itself. For in those happenings, you will have messages, and you can be assured that the messages are from your life guide or orchestrated by your life guide. For example, your life guide may be the one to guide you away from danger or guide you into something that will be quite enriching for you. It is true that loved ones who have passed on and Angels and other entities can guide, but it is often the case that your life guide is at the center of what is occurring for you while on the EarthPlane.

Does it take faith to believe you have a life guide? Of course, it does. As mentioned, you needn't know your life guide is with you to benefit from the intuitive messages he or she gives you. However, if you wish to fully benefit from your life guide's experience and assistance, it helps to become aware of their presence.

We are here to assure you that if you do proceed with great faith and trust in your ability to have that connection—then it will happen. So, read on knowing that if you choose to have a deep and personal connection with your life guide, you only need to ask. And there are a few simple steps that will increase your awareness of their presence.

1. Close your eyes and ask your life guide to be present.
2. Listen with all your senses for the "message" that he or she brings forth. The message may be very mild. It could be a slight breeze or a slight "knowing" or a whisper sensation in your ear. It is important to be open to how the message appears.
3. If at first you do not sense your life guide, don't despair. Simply stop for a moment and repeat the process at a later time.
4. Consider also that your life guide may suddenly appear at what might seem like a random time. This requires being open for the experience to suddenly occur. When it does occur, it will be anything but random—but will come at the divine right time.
5. If you still aren't able to access your life guide, consider trying a guided meditation or prepare a meditation for yourself and then use it to access your life guide.
6. During these steps, remind yourself that your life guide does exist, which will help ensure you have success at some point.

Can you access your soul purpose and ascend without consciously accessing your life guide? As mentioned, your life guide will guide you—even if you aren't aware of that guidance. So yes—you can ascend and fulfill your soul purpose without consciously "knowing" and experiencing your life guide. Therefore, don't concern yourself with this aspect if you are unable to "hear from" him or her. Continue to try to do so, and in time, you likely will. We mention life guides here, because they are an essential part of the connection between the Light and the EarthPlane.

Are there barriers that may crop up when you attempt to access your life guide? We will say this with as much tact as possible. The only barrier to accessing your life guide is you—that is, your EarthPlane consciousness. If there is any resistance in this area, even subconsciously, there will be difficulties. For that reason, it may be helpful to use a guided meditation to bring about a meeting with your life guide. Through guided meditation, you will be able to enter an altered twilight state that will reduce resistance, lower the veil between the Light and Earth-Plane, and allow for more effective communing with your guide. (See the "Stay Enlightened" page at the end of the book for an opportunity to get a free guided meditation to meet your life guide.)

PAST LIVES AND PARALLEL LIVES AND THEIR SIGNIFICANCE TO YOUR SOUL JOURNEY

Your past and parallel lifetimes on the EarthPlane are of vital importance to your soul journey. While we cannot cover these in great detail here, they are fascinating in their own right, so we will touch upon their significance and how they affect your soul ascension—for their effects are profound.

PAST LIVES

Past lifetimes are those you have lived on Earth prior to your current lifetime on the EarthPlane. These are known as reincarnations—meaning rebirths in a new body and life. They are not rebirths of your soul in any way, for your soul journey remains fluid—as one infinite river that meanders and flows and never ceases.

Your past lives consist of your various "visits" to the Earth-Plane. They vary greatly in the length of time that you stay, the "parts" that you play, and the EarthPlane experiences you undergo. One way in which they don't vary, however, is that the essence of your soul is present in all the human characters you play. This is known as the "energetic signature" of your soul. It is an energetic stamp of a sort that allows other souls to identify you without needing any other information. In current terminology, you could think of it as the hard drive of your soul. It contains your Soul DNA. This refers to your energetic, soul imprint that consists of interlocking soul strands. The strands are energetically coded in a way that creates you—your unique essence and way of being. There is much to this but suffice it to say that your Soul DNA coding represents the whole and entirety of you and is unlike any other Soul DNA that exists. As in human DNA, there are similarities that exist, of course. But there is no exact replica of you.

We mention your Soul DNA and energetic signature because they are of significance in what happens in your various lifetimes on the EarthPlane, including the emergence of lessons and experiences as you continue to ascend. Your energetic signature also allows you to connect and commune on the EarthPlane with souls with whom you already have a connection in the Light. It is a sort of guiding light that attracts souls to one another when in human form. Of course, this is something that many souls have no idea is occurring, but it is so.

Those souls who have ascended sufficiently while in human form, may and often do tap into the energetic signature of other souls. For instance, gifted physics and mediums on the EarthPlane can readily identify a soul thanks to that soul's energetic signature. They do not need anything else to help them identify the soul. That is how powerful the energetic signature is—for it is the "summation" of the soul's lives—while also encompassing the soul's true essence.

So how, then, do our past lives affect our lifetimes on the EarthPlane?

Past lifetimes resonate within one's soul when one is on the EarthPlane. While these past lifetimes affect our souls while in the Light, this is nowhere near how much they will affect us while on the EarthPlane. This is because—not surprisingly—they are past lifetimes that are Earthbound. Therefore, their significance is tied to what occurs on the Earth. However, as you will have seen, there is always a convergence of what is Earthbound and the Light. For what we experience in human form resonates and affects our soul's trajectory.

It is often believed that all is set in stone in terms of what will occur on a soul's path on the EarthPlane, but this is not the case. For there are other souls with whom we set up agreements, and those souls do not always "come through" and do as they had agreed when we were together in the Light making plans. This is due to "Earthbound amnesia" of souls about what they had intended to do when they came to Earth—and more importantly, because of free will.

Lessons gleaned while in a certain reincarnation or reincarnations on the EarthPlane can continue themes that will affect a soul's trajectory while on the EarthPlane, and that in turn will affect a soul's ascension in and out of the Light.

Suffice it to say the convergence in this way between the EarthPlane and the Light is complex and continuous, and the way in which past lives affect the soul's ascension is of great significance. For these lives are steppingstones or rungs on the ladder on one's ascension journey.

Does this refer to "negative" past lifetimes where there was much strife and want and need? Yes, it does. But it also refers to past lifetimes that were quite grand and powerful and uplifting and even magnificent. It is often thought that you only learn from the tough lessons of life while in human form. But, in fact, much is learned from what those in human form would call "the beautiful moments." These moments also resonate deeply with a soul's trajectory—given the nature of the great power that all souls have while in the Light. Certainly, this is a power that a soul always has at his or her "fingertips," but because of Earthbound amnesia, one would not know this. So, in every way, past lifetimes build upon each other to facilitate a soul's ascension.

EARTHBOUND AMNESIA

Before we move onto parallel lives, which are an intriguing concept, we will mention Earthbound amnesia. It is important you also understand this concept, because it has a direct and lasting impact on your soul ascension journey and especially your experiences while on the EarthPlane.

Earthbound amnesia refers to the fact that when souls leave the LightPlane for the EarthPlane after making intricate plans for their time to be spent on Earth, they lose memory of the fact that they are of and from the Light and especially lose memory of the plans they made for themselves while in human form.

We know that at first glance this seems contradictory and even at cross purposes as to what a soul is attempting to accomplish while on the EarthPlane. For wouldn't you want to know your agenda while you are here? Wouldn't it be much more efficient and satisfying to have a wonderful template as to what to do, say, and be—so that you can ascend more rapidly and with less inter-ference?

You have heard us speak of free will quite often, and this concept does fit in here. The top law of the Universe, as mentioned, is free will. This is the top law on the EarthPlane, also. That being said, free will is an aspect that could not and would not come forward should an Earthbound soul know his or her plan for the duration while on the EarthPlane. For then the Earth-Plane experience would not be the experience it becomes. It would instead be just like the LightPlane existence and of no value to a soul's expansion. We say this because the energy on the Earth-Plane is of a much lower vibration than in the Light.

Let us share an analogy with you that will help you grasp this concept. If you were to know what you had planned to do and all others you know also know this, you would simply be on a continual merry-go-round repeating the same dull, repetitive experiences. What makes the EarthPlane the "training ground" it is for the soul are its many, many, many varied experiences. All those experiences are borne of free will—via yourself while in your current reincarnation of you, and via others and their free will while in their current reincarnation.

It is important to mention there are other souls on the Earth-Plane who have connections with you through your past and parallel lifetimes together. What they choose to do or not do in response to their Earthbound amnesia greatly affects your soul journey while on the EarthPlane.

You may be thinking at this point, "I and others I know are aware of some of the things meant to be accomplished during our meeting on the EarthPlane." This is most certainly true, and something a soul can tap into and access via meditation and consulting with spiritual advisors. If you are particularly tapped in, these visions and intuitive thoughts may come to you from the Light. Yet, you may notice that your entire plan does not present itself clearly before you when you access this information. Rather, you will receive pieces of information parceled out to you. This parceling out occurs as your higher self/soul allows, because you are meant to learn lessons by not being able to access certain information until it is time. Otherwise, the EarthPlane existence, as mentioned, would be of no consequence or use to your soul ascension. Yes, the EarthPlane existence can be enjoyable, but that is not the only reason you come to the Earth in various reincarnations. As mentioned by us quite often, the purpose of the soul is to ascend, and the EarthPlane offers a plethora of options for doing so.

PARALLEL LIVES

Now we will delve into parallel lifetimes, which are lesser known, yet equally as vital to your EarthPlane journey and its significance to your ascension.

First, a definition of parallel lifetimes. These are lifetimes you are living in tandem (parallel) with your current lifetime. They are not to be confused with past lifetimes, for they aren't technically in the past. Rather, they are running concurrently with your current lifetime. We know this can be a confusing concept, but as mentioned, these lifetimes are vital to your soul ascension as it relates to the EarthPlane. There are a few rules about these lifetimes to consider. Then we will cover how these experiences affect your soul ascension as it relates to the EarthPlane.

Parallel lifetimes have a few rules—one of them being that a soul cannot run into a parallel life in this lifetime. By this we mean that if you are living a life as a physician in Australia, let's say, and a lifetime in America as a professor—neither would encounter the other in this lifetime. The forces at work would never allow this to happen. So, if you are concerned about this happening, you need not be. It is also important to note that not every soul in human form is living parallel lifetimes. Sometimes a soul is living just one all-consuming lifetime and this is more than enough to ensure progress on ascension at the present time.

REASONS WHY SOULS CHOOSE PARALLEL LIFETIMES

The most important reason for parallel lifetimes is to further the soul's ultimate goal of ascension. For instance, a soul may decide to have lifetimes that mirror one another in struggles and lessons. This is the case when the soul wishes to amplify a particular lesson. For instance, perhaps the person is suffering physically in both lifetimes. These lifetimes mirror one another and make the lesson more profound and more likely to teach what was intended.

Parallel lifetimes also afford the opportunity to learn dual lessons. For instance, perhaps a soul wishes to learn lessons in patience while also learning lessons in acting on one's desires, rather than waiting. These are somewhat contrary lessons. Therefore, it helps to be able to live dual existences at the same time, with each focused on one of those lessons.

Parallel lifetimes speed up the ascension process for those

souls who wish to learn greater and greater lessons. This is something that comes about naturally as a matter of course. The amplification process and the ability to learn different lessons at the same time ensure this occurs.

Parallel lifetimes afford a soul the ability to stretch even further. As mentioned, the EarthPlane is a soul "training ground" that offers very serious, hard-knock lessons. Great ability is required in juxtaposing various parallel existences and living out those lessons concurrently.

HOW PARALLEL LIFETIMES AFFECT SOUL GROWTH

Now we will comment on how these parallel lifetime existences affect your overall soul ascension and how they relate to the convergence between the LightPlane and the EarthPlane. All lessons in and out of the Light are lessons that afford a soul with growth opportunities. That being said, there are lessons on the EarthPlane that can be learned through parallel lives. Such lifetimes are a higher-order type of tool that can be experimented with on the EarthPlane and the effects monitored from within the Light.

Parallel lifetimes are a tool that are only sometimes employed. There are various reasons for this. For one, it is hard on the physical, mental, and spiritual bodies of the soul in human form. For two, it is difficult for a soul in human form to absorb all the intended lessons when living a dual existence, because of physical and mental stressors. For three, when one does split in more than one direction, one risks each of the lifetimes becoming so difficult that the entire mission of learning simultaneous lessons is aborted. This is not to say that juggling more than one lifetime can't be accomplished. It is only to say that it doesn't always work as intended. Then again, not every lifetime and the intended lessons do "work," even when the lifetime is a singular one. We do hear you wondering how that is possible, for isn't all that is planned in the Light followed through on by one's soul? Yes and no.

When it comes to the convergence and interaction between the LightPlane and the EarthPlane, things do not always work out as intended. Does this mean they will never work out, no matter how well-intended a soul may be? Not necessarily. In fact, most souls do continue to repeat a lesson in various formulations until that lesson is absorbed and assimilated. Does that mean you will return with your mother each lifetime if you are intended to learn a lesson with her? It could mean that, or it could mean that someone else steps in to help you learn that particular lesson in the next lifetime, should it not get learned in the present one.

Why your mother may not step back into the spot will have to do with her soul's many soul purposes and schedules. Much like on the EarthPlane, a soul may be scheduled to do something else when you plan to return for the same lesson. Yes, that person could potentially live a parallel lifetime if you are both to be on the EarthPlane at the same time, but your mother may not have the bandwidth to do so, depending on her intended lifetime. Conversely, you may not have written your new script to include the exact same lesson. You may have tweaked the lesson so that you accomplish what you set out to do in a different manner— one that you feel you'll be more likely to accomplish while in human form.

All this said, it is critical as you are likely intuiting that other souls agree to work with us on our various soul missions. The best and most common situation is when both souls can gain lessons from one another while in human form. This will mean that you will be gaining valuable lessons with your mother as she is also learning lessons. If you look at the various relationships in your life and what has occurred between you and those key people, you will often see that the other person is gaining as many lessons as you.

It is also important to mention at this juncture that lessons beget lessons. By this we mean that you will learn a particular lesson and then will decide when in the Light that you would like to return to Earth to drill down further on that lesson. For instance, say that you have decided to learn a lesson in compassion. You come to the EarthPlane with a "lesson plan" in place that includes a career as a humanitarian. Once done with that lesson, which may have been in macro terms, you may decide to come back in another lifetime to drill down even further and learn the lesson in a microenvironment. You could, for instance, come back and parent a child with disabilities. You can see how such a life situation would give you ample opportunities to learn compassion.

Monitoring a Soul's Ascension Process while on the EarthPlane from the Light

It stands to reason that a soul's ascension process would be monitored while the soul is in human form on the EarthPlane. But who does the monitoring? While on the EarthPlane, many believe there is a higher power/being monitoring from the Light. However, the truth is that one's higher self does the monitoring and is one's "higher power." Yes, that means that you monitor you.

But how can that be, you may ask? Isn't that like self-editing? Yes, it is, and who better to "edit" you than you? This is not to say you don't consult with others during your soul ascension and even confer with others about your soul ascension progress while on Earth. This most certainly occurs with your life guide and other guides, including Ascended Masters and Angels and Archangels. But it does point out the fact that we are all one with self—and therefore we are all in charge of self.

Yes, we are all interconnected, but we are all our own selves, and we connect as our whole selves with others' whole selves. Of course, here we are speaking of connecting within the Light, for while on the EarthPlane, many souls do diverge from the Oneness of Self as they strive to make themselves feel better/good by latching onto another soul. While this paradigm is most certainly a soul's prerogative, and in many cases a soul's lesson, it does not occur in the Light. We are all one whole and in no need to latch onto other souls while in the Light.

The latter being said, are there souls on the EarthPlane at this moment seeking to strive toward Oneness of Self rather than merging with another? Yes, there are. Is this even possible, however, while in human form? Yes, it is. However, this is a higher order lesson not many pursue. Why, you may ask, if this lesson is one that will elevate a soul tremendously don't more souls attempt this? One, of course, because it is very difficult to do in human form. The other reason being that this is something a soul would do once a soul has ascended tremendously. So, if you are reading this and you seem to be attempting this Oneness of Self, know at this juncture you are an extremely ascended soul.

What should you do with this information? Suffice it to say you have heard this now to explain to you why you have struggled with this lesson, and to know you are on the right path. Of course, your path will be quite different from another's path, and yet, you will struggle with the same human emotions and actions surrounding this very difficult lesson.

We know this is a bit of a heady lesson here—this connecting with others as our whole selves, free and clear to not attempt to latch on to others in order to feel "complete and content."

Back to monitoring one's Soul Ascension Path while on the EarthPlane from the Light. How does this process look for a soul? Here is what occurs when you monitor yourself from the Light while on the EarthPlane.

1. The higher self/soul does the monitoring. Think of this as a captain on his or her "starship." There is an observation deck from which the soul keeps an eye on the progress of the soul while in human form. The part of the soul in human form is the lower self and the part of the soul in the Light is the higher self. The

lower self is created to live out a human existence on the EarthPlane. The lower self does not appear anywhere else in the Multiverse. From this observation deck, the higher self monitors every aspect of the soul's human form existence. This ranges from what may seem very mundane, such as how you brush your teeth, to epiphanies regarding your soul journey.

2. The observation is recorded in what we will describe and explain here as a LightPlane box. Think of this as a box containing information about one's soul journey. Within that box you will find a hard drive of sorts that is continually recording the soul journey while on the EarthPlane. The contents of the hard drive are organized in a fashion that allows for instantaneous sorting of events, occurrences, epiphanies, realizations, learning points, turning points, and conclusions to lessons. Of course, the box is not a solid mass as you would find on the EarthPlane. Rather, it is an energetic assortment of what we have just mentioned. We use the analogy of a hard drive, because digital records are more like what we are explaining to you than hard copies.

3. What is done with all this information? Much like what might occur if you uploaded information from a hard drive to another device, the same occurs when your EarthPlane existence data is collected. In short, it is uploaded to the soul. There the data is sorted and tested and analyzed—all in an instantaneous method that could be likened to what occurs with a computer program. After the sifting and sorting of the data is complete and the information is placed in various quadrants, the soul then decides what to do with the data while also using the information toward soul ascension. We hear you asking if someone else—a

deity perhaps—reviews and approves the data. Once again, we must repeat that the soul is in charge of the soul. While this varies a bit when the soul is on the EarthPlane, because a life guide is also involved, a soul is in charge of itself while in the Light. The life guide is needed while the soul is on the EarthPlane due to Earthbound amnesia, much like a person with vision problems requires a seeing eye dog.

4. Monitoring of the physical is also done from the Light. While this may seem odd in a way, as the soul does not have to worry about the physical, it is of vital importance, as the soul must ensure that the human body does not wear out or down prior to the accomplishment of the soul mission. That being said, the soul keeps an eye on the human body and its functioning, including vital organs and limbs and important things like the eyes, ears, etc. We know that some souls come to the EarthPlane to learn physical lessons. For instance, they may come to experience a lifetime of physical discomfort and pain, while other souls may come for mental suffering. Whatever the type of suffering occurring, the soul is monitoring the body and the effects on the body from the Light. This is why at times there will be divine intervention where a soul may be cured of an ailment/physical condition so that the human body can go on. This does occur in near-death experiences, which we have covered earlier in the book. At times, the physical body may be partially healed so that the person may go on, yet still get the physical lesson. As we have mentioned previously, the lessons are all individual and quite different from one another, although there will be similarities.

5. There is no grading system used when monitoring a soul's progress and experience on the EarthPlane. It is

important to understand that for souls in the Light
there is never a race against time as you will find on
the EarthPlane, for there is no real time. Only
stretches of energy within which souls exist—and
these stretches of energy expand and contract as
needed.

If you hear the testimonies of those who have had near-death
experiences and go to the Light temporarily—you will sometimes
hear how time seemed to shrink and contract for them. For while
they were effectively dead in the human physical sense—their
spirit or soul endured. And they will have a hard time explaining
that time did not seem to exist and yet it did exist. For this reason,
we have chosen to say that time seems to "stretch"—as in a flash
of light or even lightning. You will remember that lightning and
thunder do not light up and sound simultaneously—even though
they are formed together at the same time. You see the lightning
and then hear the thunder.

Why are we discussing so thoroughly this concept of time on
the EarthPlane and in the Light? Because in the Light there is no
real sense of time. Time matters to humans, and in many respects
time can be of the utmost importance to you. For you come to the
EarthPlane in a human body to live a human existence that is
finite. This is not something that occurs in the Light—only on
the EarthPlane. Therefore "time" has meaning for humans. Even
reading and digesting the words in this book will take a certain
amount of time, and you must allot the time to do this. Furthermore, our Master Channeler on the EarthPlane—in order to
channel this book from the Light to you—had to make a certain
amount of time available, and schedules were created and adhered
to in the Light and on the EarthPlane for this to happen.

SIGNIFICANCE OF DIVINE TIMING

It is vital you understand the concept of Divine Timing. We cannot say this often enough or more emphatically. On the Earth-Plane, the human tendency is to wish, want, desire, and demand that things happen either more quickly than they do, or at a specific time. However, wishing, wanting, desiring, demanding, or stomping your feet does not bring about the desired changes any faster, and in fact, can slow down the process considerably. So that is why we wish you to understand and embrace Divine Timing, because it truly is your "friend."

Speaking further on this concept of Divine Timing being your friend—we think you will agree that when events occur in your life and you reach goals and milestones of importance to you, you can often look back and see that if you had reached those milestones and goals sooner, things would not have worked out as seamlessly or as well—and sometimes not worked out at all. For the truth is, you create EarthPlane lesson plans and their intended results with other souls. Therefore, it is essential you wait for those other souls to follow through on what you have all agreed upon.

You will often hear souls who meet one another on the Earth-Plane recount their earlier years and how they couldn't have met one another any sooner, due to a variety of circumstances. Perhaps because one of them was located in a different geographic area at that time. So, we urge you to embrace and allow Divine Timing to be at play in your life. For the outcome will occur no matter what you do. You can kick and scream and pout and moan and groan about it, or you can simply accept it for what it is and enjoy what is right in front of you. It is your choice. What is not your choice is when or whether the other souls you have chosen to align with step up and do what has been agreed upon. There is therefore a need for all souls involved to align in their common purpose, and when circumstances come together in such a way, all the pieces fall into place in the "Divine Right Time."

WHEN TIME ON THE EARTHPLANE CONVERGES WITH TIME IN THE LIGHT

When there is a convergence of time on the EarthPlane and time in the Light, it can be cataclysmic. This convergence occurs when the two types of time meet. This particularly applies to Divine Timing, where there can be a bit of an ah-ha moment, or even a "what on earth just happened to my life?" moment. If you understand the convergence, then when Divinely Timed occurrences happen, you will feel them to your very core, and you will simply "know." At the same time, you may be a bit dumbstruck or feel blindsided—which are common reactions.

Time can and does stretch and shrink on the EarthPlane. This is an occurrence that you may or may not notice. Perhaps you recall times when you were working on something or enjoying a conversation with another person and the time seemed to stretch, while at other times, the time seemed to disappear in an instant. This is what we mean by the stretching and shrinking of time.

The stretching and shrinking is of significance when you are otherwise occupied by a task or goal. In particular, the stretching of time is significant if you are attempting to make progress or finish a step toward your soul purpose. For example, in the creation of this book, time has stretched on occasion for the author in order to get the words down on the page for you to read, despite other time constraints.

In addition, we would be remiss not to mention how time can and will shrink. You may be wondering why on earth you would want time to shrink. The fact is that there may be difficult occurrences in your life, and there are times when you wish for something to end as soon as possible. In those instances, once the experience is no longer serving you, time will indeed shrink, and the experience will end. It may be incremental and barely visible, but then again, it may be as if it ended all of a sudden. Either way, there is a "manipulation" of time, which is the best way to explain it.

Who manipulates the time, you may be wondering? Often it is your team in the Light—those souls/beings/entities at your disposal to help you with all your soul purpose initiatives. However, it is of the utmost importance for you to understand you are in charge of all of those initiatives. You have decided how and when you need time shrinkage or time expansion, and those at your disposal "make" it happen.

How does the actual convergence reveal itself on the Earth-Plane and can it be experienced?

The convergence of time in the Light and time on the Earth-Plane can be cataclysmic—similar to lightning hitting a tree. Conversely, the collision of time can be mild and barely noticeable. The question is, what is the reason for the collision of time, and why has it happened in the first place?

If the reason for the collision is to stop something from happening—for instance, a planned event is no longer desired—then the collision can be somewhat abrupt. Picture, for example, a car coming to a complete stop very quickly to avoid entering an intersection and plowing into another vehicle. That is how an abrupt about-face with time colliding on the EarthPlane and Light would look. Something that was planned is suddenly aborted. On the flip side, the "collision" may be nearly imperceptible. For instance, if you were thinking about having orange juice but decided to drink milk, instead. We think you see what we are saying here, even though the concept of time and its fluidity is not an easy one to embrace and understand.

Speaking of the fluidity of time, let us use an analogy. Consider that time in the Light is much like waves in the ocean. Time ebbs and flows and meanders and is overpowered by the various agendas and initiatives of souls within the Light. This begs another question, which is, are there different notions of time for different souls? Yes, there are. Using the ocean analogy will help you grasp this concept, as the flow of water seems to have no rhyme or reason—yet when one studies oceanography and the ocean floor and how the ocean affects climate and weather patterns across the globe, you begin to understand that there is indeed a rhyme and a reason to it all.

Many on the EarthPlane would like to grasp tightly onto time and even slow or stall time. This can be seen in those who cling to certain circumstances that are occurring—for instance their professions or relationships. While this need to cling is certainly understandable from a human perspective, you know at a soul level that on the EarthPlane time does "march on," and clinging must end at some point. The EarthPlane human body does age. While there are certainly ways to encourage the human body to remain fit and to last longer, it will eventually run its course.

We remind you here that the soul in the Light never ages. The soul remains as youthful as it was when it first "sparked" into being. However, the soul does mature. By this we mean that the soul ascends and learns lesson upon lesson in the Light and out of the Light in other dimensions—one of which is the EarthPlane. This is an important distinction, and one that you may have difficulty grasping as an Earthbound soul at this time. An analogy may help you understand. Let us think of an Earthbound item such as wine or certain cheeses. They remain youthful in their flavor profile, while at the same time they mature in a sense, as they are aged to create the various nuances within the flavor profile that make them sought after and even coveted—in particular in the case of wine.

We wish to emphasize that "time" is only one construct on the EarthPlane. Often, humans wish to cling to time as the "only" construct to ensure order. But in so doing, too much emphasis is placed on time. For instance, this occurs in the form of striving to complete goals, missions, activities, and tasks on "schedule," and in regard to how long something or someone will "last." This approach, however, limits and inhibits your potential enjoyment of the EarthPlane existence. We urge you to pay less attention to "time," and more attention to other aspects of your life, such as your relationships with others and your connection with Source/the Light/your higher self and the resulting "meaning of life," as you like to call it. For time truly does not exist in the Light. And if you play your cards right, to use an EarthPlane expression, time does not need to mean so much to you during your stay on Earth.

Of course, you do have to pay some attention to time, for matters such as getting to work in a punctual manner and paying your bills on time, but in the scheme of things, these are a minute part of what people on the EarthPlane tend to worry about with regard to time. Rather, they fret about being a year older and become concerned they are running out of time to get done what they think they need to get done and wanted to get done. Conversely, they may feel they have finished with the EarthPlane and are ready to go home to the Light, and yet, they are still here.

We wish you to be at peace with time—with Divine Time. We assure you that when you do, you will more fully enjoy and understand and embrace the EarthPlane experience. And you will be ready when your time comes to return to the Light.

You do not come to the EarthPlane simply to enjoy the "limited" time to which you often refer. For a great part of being on Earth is simply to enjoy existing in such a space with the ability "to just be." If you can remind yourself of the possibility of your transcending what may be considered the norm on the EarthPlane and simply know and realize you are able to come here from the Light simply to "exist" without a thought as to for how long and even the type of experiences you may have, but simply to be in awe of the fact that you can reincarnate and come to the Earth-Plane directly from the Light, then you will discover an inner knowing and sense of awe in the realization that "you are you"—a completely unique being—and part of a greater collective within the Universe.

We urge you to reflect upon this understanding on a daily basis, for doing so will give you a sense of calm and a profound understanding of your own being and your reason for existing—both in the Light and on the EarthPlane during your current incarnation.

COMMUNICATING WITH THE OTHER SIDE WHILE IN HUMAN FORM

It should come as no surprise that souls communicate while in human form with the Other Side/the Light. This is obviously required so that you can continue with your soul purpose while armed with vital facts as to what to do next and what not to do.

The vehicle for humans communicating with the Other Side is their higher self. As mentioned previously, the higher self is that part of you—your inner essence or soul—that always resides in the Light and is therefore privy to all you had planned to do while in your current incarnation and the achievements you desired for your lower self's journey on the EarthPlane. The higher self is your principal guide for your lower self's journey while you are on the EarthPlane. Your life guide on the EarthPlane also participates in guiding—to assist you to grow.

So, how does this communication occur between your higher and lower self? For some individuals, such as Julie, who is channeling this book, communicating with her higher self is straightforward, as she is clairaudient and can hear what her higher self is saying and suggesting, and sometimes insisting upon.

But what about the rest of humanity and those souls who may not hear direct suggestions and directives? This is where claircognizance comes into play. This term refers to using intuition and gut feelings to tap into what feels right for yourself in terms of what to do and not to do, and the steps to be taken to bring this about. Most humans accept this form of guidance from their lower self—usually without realizing this is occurring.

Many humans communicate with their higher selves while they are asleep. This occurs in the form of meetings that you attend in the Light. Sometimes these are with just your higher self and sometimes with your higher self and the higher selves of others. You may know that you've met with your higher self when you go to bed with a question in your mind about something that may be bothering or puzzling you, and then wake up with a brilliant answer. That is an indication that you went to the Light while asleep and had a good session with yourself and potentially with others. Meetings with others often occur if what is causing you consternation involves more than yourself.

There are those who believe that the human mind's subconscious is responsible for solving problems seemingly overnight. That can be the case, but often the higher self weighs in and makes the final decisions. This begs the question as to the difference between the subconscious and the higher self. The easiest way to explain this is that the subconscious is Earth-Plane-based and located only within this incarnation of you. Think of the subconscious as part of your Earthbound brain. It can go no further than what is occurring for you at this moment in time in this lifetime. Your higher self, on the other hand, is privy to everything about your soul and your soul journey.

What about the meetings with your higher self in the Light? Are these formal meetings? Or less formal and fleeting? They are all of the above, depending on your needs at that particular point in time. For example, you may need to complete a project rather quickly. In that case, you wouldn't have time for a long, involved meeting. Rather, you would require speedy information to help you move on with your project.

At the other end of the spectrum, you might have an intensive and extensive project you estimate will take you much time to complete. In that case, a meeting with your higher self to lay out the details and come up with a plan of action would be in order.

There are various ways receiving messages from your higher self will take place. You may simply be guided to the answer and have the urge to do something in response. Another way we have already mentioned is that you will "sleep on" the issue/problem/challenge and wake up in the morning ready to tackle things. Many would say your subconscious worked on the problem while you slept. The fact is that your lower and higher selves worked on the problem together. Your higher self offered solutions, and your lower self embraced those solutions, with the aim of making them a reality.

What of issues that don't seem to have a solution? What then? Would your higher and lower selves disagree, for example, about how to deal with the issue? This is a rather nuanced situation and as such has a nuanced answer.

First of all, it is important to understand that your higher and lower selves are always at one, according to your life purpose and where you are going. We can see this raising some eyebrows, for in human form you sometimes do things you consider against your higher self's direct advice. While this is sometimes the case, at the same time we remind you that you came to the EarthPlane to learn, which you do every minute of every day. As such, you will "go against" the wisdom of your higher self on purpose. By that we mean you may resist advice to learn lessons. By going against your higher self's suggestions/advice, you end up having a "consequence."

This is not to say you wouldn't already have a consequence by going with your higher self's advice. But generally speaking, when you go against what you "just knew" to do or not do, the fallout is generally more dramatic and messy. We think you see what we are saying here. And with the fallout, you learn the richest lessons.

However, your lower self never really disagrees with your higher self. You may resist what your higher self is saying to do, but you both know that your higher plan—located within your higher self in the Light—is what serves you and the Greater Good.

Balking at what you know you should do is quite common. For example, if an authority figure advises you to do something and you know it is the best course of action, but you also know the task will be difficult and may take a long time by EarthPlane standards, you might seek a shortcut. However, by not doing what has been requested or ordered, you don't get the benefits of what would have transpired had you done so. There is the same sort of connection and interchange between your higher and lower selves. Your higher self may suggest saying or doing something, but perhaps it is an unpleasant task, or would take quite a bit of dedication and work. You respond by delaying fulfilling the request—or downright refusing. While it might seem as if by refusing you could "get out of" doing whatever is requested or ordered by your higher self, this generally isn't the case. What does occur, however, is that you will be uncomfortable and may even experience pain from not following directions. That is not "the worst of it," however. The lesson will come back again in another form if you don't finally heed the request/order. And the next time the consequences may be more severe. This cycle generally continues until you give in and heed the request/order. And then what happens? Things begin to run more smoothly for you.

Is the message from this to listen to your higher self directives and simply heed them? Yes, that is the overall message. However, if you haven't heeded orders previously, refrain from beating yourself up over it. Because not heeding the directives teaches you as many, if not more, lessons. Not following through on what you know you should do is a grand teacher—providing you do eventually heed the messages and follow through. Of course, not everyone does that. Does that mean they need to come back in another lifetime to learn the lessons? We will now cover this matter.

THE IDEA OF RETURNING TO LEARN LESSONS

The concept that if you do not fulfill your soul purpose you must come back to the EarthPlane to do so is a pervasive one within spiritual ideology on the EarthPlane. We will touch on this aspect and make things clearer to you in this area.

If you are not familiar with this concept, it says that if you "fail" to follow through on certain elements of your soul purpose journey, you must reincarnate and try again. As we have often said here—yes and no.

Firstly, as mentioned before, "failing" is sometimes "succeeding." By this we are referring to not doing something you know you should do so that you can then learn valuable lessons. This could mean you are actually succeeding with your soul purpose. We think you understand what we are saying here.

That then begs the question: If you fail to fully achieve your supposed soul purpose but learn lessons during the "failing," have you truly failed? The answer is no. We would instead say that you have succeeded. As you can see, this is a very complex terrain—this "succeeding" or "failing" at soul purpose initiatives. We are not saying that you wouldn't necessarily come back in another incarnation if you didn't reach a certain summit or apex during your soul journey, and yet, you might not. As we have mentioned in this book, every soul's journey is unique. No two souls are ever the same. That means that each soul journey, and whether you need to return and "do it over again," is unique to that person.

It is of the utmost importance that you continue to strive for your soul purpose with every reincarnation. That is what we would like you to internalize. You may return to try to learn a lesson again, and then again you may decide during your time in the Light between Earthbound lives that you no longer need that lesson—or more likely, that you no longer need that exact lesson. You may decide you need the lesson with minor or major tweaks. This "altering as you go" is all part of each soul's unique ascension journey.

What do you understand from all of this? We want you to know that you do not need to be overly concerned with having to return to learn lessons, if you don't learn them in your current incarnation. While we have likened your soul ascension journey to the educational system, we assure you that you won't be held back in kindergarten indefinitely! It is a more complex system and process and is uniquely suited to you. It is also important to note that you won't feel the discomfort of returning to refine the lesson. Instead, you will be eager to return—much like a kindergarten child running onto the playground during recess!

THE SOLO SOUL JOURNEY

As was mentioned in the final section of Part One in this book—though souls do come together to accomplish great things on the EarthPlane—in the end, a soul enters and leaves the EarthPlane alone—for the soul journey is essentially a solo one. Yes, you will team up with many other souls along your soul journey, and with some for long periods of time by EarthPlane standards. But at the end of each reincarnation of you, and always within the Light, you are your own unique person. Your goals, lessons, accomplishments, and epiphanies are yours and yours alone.

We can hear you thinking, but my partner has been with me for many years and is such an integral part of my journey. Certainly, this doesn't apply to me! To be frank—yes, it does. This person has augmented your soul journey and even greatly influenced it, but at some point, one of you will leave the other on the EarthPlane. At the same time, you will never leave each other in the Light. However—this is an important distinction—within the Light there is a definite, distinct separation between souls. It is not a separation that souls notice or are bothered by. On the contrary, it is how all souls are meant to be—essentially solo. We know this is difficult for those of you who are entwined with another soul—or wish to be. We are not saying you cannot climb the proverbial ascension ladder with others. Just know that they will be on their own ladder beside you—not on the same ladder.

We don't wish to belabor this point, but we do want to share that the sooner you can accept the fact that your soul journey is truly solo and that you can rise all on your own and scale great heights all by yourself, the sooner you will ascend more rapidly. And the sooner you will tap into the deep, abiding faith in your soul and your soul journey that can and does make each reincarnation on the EarthPlane an exhilarating and joyful adventure.

* * *

You have now read our account of the union of the Light and the Earth at exactly the right moment for you on your Soul Ascension journey.

We hope you have enjoyed learning more about how the Light and the EarthPlane embrace and complement each other, and that you continue to enjoy the inspiration and exhilaration of living out your unique purpose within the Universe.

Namaste

Bhagwan (Maitreya), et al.

Glossary

Archangels: Leaders of the Angels who are part of the Seraphim. Each Archangel has specialized skills used for the betterment of the LightPlane and the EarthPlane.

Ascended Masters: Souls who dwell perpetually in the Light, yet visit the EarthPlane often to impart wisdom and knowledge to the mass of humanity.

Ascension/Ascend: To experience increasingly greater levels of enlightenment.

Channeling: Translating messages from the Light/Multiverse into written and spoken form.

Cosmos: Encompasses all realms. Also known as the Multiverse.

EarthPlane: Planet Earth where the physical body exists and resides.

Elementals: Mystical, magical beings, including fairies, elves, sprites, unicorns, mermaids and mermen, and genies.

Energetic Signature: An energetic stamp that allows other souls to identify you without needing any other information.

Essences: Vital fragments of the soul that when pulled together create the whole.

Higher Self: The spirit/soul. That part of a person that always remains in the Light, yet affects the actions of the Lower Self.

Life Map: A map of your journey on Earth for a reincarnation.

LightPlane: Realm where the soul resides and there is no physical body. (See the Light).

Lower Self: The part of the soul in human form responsible for the Earthbound physical body and its actions and inactions.

Mind Map: The view or map of a "soul's journey" as it is imprinted in that soul's mind. The mind map changes over time in some respects, but in many respects it stays the same from lifetime to lifetime.

Multiverse: Encompasses all realms. Also known as Cosmos.

Realms: Those locations within the Multiverse where "life" resides. This includes the LightPlane and EarthPlane.

Seraphim: Highest order of Angels that sit at the right hand of the Archangels and are comprised of very high-level energy nearly impossible to see by the naked human eye.

Soul: Your spirit/very being that always endures.

Soul DNA: Energetic, soul imprint that consists of interlocking soul strands. The strands are energetically coded in a way that creates you—your unique essence and way of being. There is much to this but suffice it to say that your Soul DNA coding represents the whole and entirety of you and is unlike any other Soul DNA that exists. As in human DNA, there are similarities that exist, of course. But there is no exact replica of you.

Soul Journey: This refers to the journey, which is neverending, of a soul. It is the mapping of the soul's complete and often complex journey from the soul spark stage and onwards. Each human lifetime is included in this soul journey, as well as all the other learning and "ascension pinpoints" along the way.

Soul Map: A roadmap of all your plans for ascension. While it contains many set points for your soul, at the same time it is a real-time, work-in-progress type of energetic document that has no end.

Spark: Point when each soul is created or born.

The Divine: The community in the Light and the Light-Plane overall.

The Light: Realm that all those currently not in human form inhabit.

Universe: The realm in which the EarthPlane and Light exists.

About the Author

Ascended Master Bhagwan Shree Rajneesh, now also known as Osho, was born in 1931 in Kuchwada, India, to fulfill the prophecy of Gautama Buddha that a World Teacher (Maitreya) would be born 2,500 years later. Bhagwan embraced the wisdom of all faiths and creeds and was available to all people on their paths toward spiritual enlightenment. He returned to the Light in 1990 and continues to share his vision from The Great Beyond. His books, videos, tapes, and presence are shared by ever-increasing millions around the world. Bhagwan's central tenets are that you cannot die, love is all there is, and you are already perfect as you are.

About the Author

Julie Bawden-Davis is a bestselling author, certified medium, healer, past life intuitive, and spiritual coach. A Master Channeler, Julie imparts messages from Spirit/The Light, including through books, written letters, and voice. She is the author of numerous works, including The Channeled Masters Series and The Channeled Insights Series. Julie's mission is to impart information and messages from the Light that heal, enlighten, and inspire, so that people can learn to trust and embrace their soul journeys, leading to joyful, healthy, abundant living.

A Note For You

Dear Enlightened Reader,

If you like this book, please leave a review or just stars on **Amazon**, **GoodReads**, **BookBub**, or all three. Your opinion matters and is incredibly powerful.

Thanks again and talk soon!

Julie

Stay Enlightened

Thanks for reading! Let's stay in touch. I post inspirational blogs on my website at https://www.juliebawdendavis.com/spiritual-coaching-blog/. You can also email me at Julie@JulieBawden Davis.com, find me on Facebook, and follow me on Amazon.

Even better, join my newsletter, *Weekly Inspirations*, and you'll receive **Divinely Inspired Messages** just for you. Sign up at: bit.ly/4iCqcND, and receive a free channeled guided meditation to access your Life Guide.

Books by Julie Bawden-Davis

The Channeled Insights Series

Mysteries of the Light Revealed: All You Want to Know about Life on the Other Side

Channeling 101: How to Access Insights from Spirit in Written and Oral Forms (coming soon)

Past and Parallel Lives: How They Affect Our Now (coming soon)

The Channeled Masters Series

Channeled Writing Tips from 111 Literary Masters

Channeled Cooking Tips from 44 Culinary Masters

Channeled Music Tips from 77 Musical Masters

Channeled Fashion Tips from 33 Master Designers and Models

The Past Life Prism Series

(Romantic Time Travel Suspense)

Suspended: The Beginning

Suspended Enforcement

Suspended Entrapment

Suspended Exodus

Suspended Entanglement

BOOKS BY JULIE BAWDEN-DAVIS

The Past Life Prism Series Box Set: Books 1-4
Suspended Control

www.ingramcontent.com/pod-product-compliance
Lightning Source LLC
Chambersburg PA
CBHW051833040426
42447CB00006B/508